D1772898

BECAUSE OF YOU...

It had always seemed so simple
When there was a cook on call
And all you did for dinner
Was to sit and eat it all.

Oh, sure, one day you too would learn
To cook and all that stuff
But other things were much more fun
And there wasn't time enough.

And before you quite realized it
It was time to leave the nest
And now you're independent
And your wings you have to test.

But your mind has suddenly gone blank
And the panic's setting in
Your tummy's grumbling for a meal
But how do you begin?

Start leafing through these pages,
And the learning's sure to come
And before you even know it
You'll be...

COOKING WITHOUT MOM!

Dedicated to all our little darlings...
Barb, Sarah, Judy, Jennifer, Rose
Sandra, Connie
Bernice, Michelle, Deana
Rob, Dave, Susan
Rick, Kevin
Bonnie, Lillian, Monica
Christopher
Wayne, Daryl, Cheryl
Steve and finally, to Dave, *who had a notion.......*

© 1986 by Hen Party Enterprises
Illustrations © by Shelley Ackerman
All rights reserved

Fifth Printing – 1994

Published by Hen Party Enterprises
2162 Crestview Crescent
Castlegar, B.C.
V1N 3B3

Mary Cheveldave	Lola Sherstobitoff
Nadeen Elasoff	Lola Tymofievich
Margaret Holuboff	Shirley Wanjoff
Mary Picton	Anne Zibin
Kathy Popoff	

Produced by
Shelley Ackerman
Robert Popoff
John Snelgrove

Printed in Canada

TABLE OF CONTENTS ━━━━━━━━

IN THE KITCHEN

SPATULAS

MEASURING
SPOONS

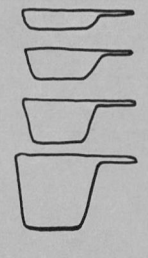

MEASURING
CUP

EGG BEATER

CASSEROLE
DISH

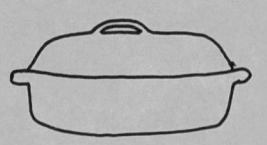

ROASTING
PAN

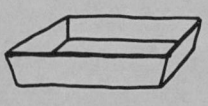

BAKING PAN

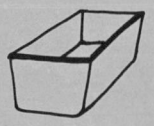

LOAF PAN

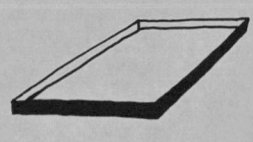

COOKIE SHEET

METRIC CONVERSION CHART ▬▬▬

COOKING MEASUREMENTS:

1 tsp.	= 5 ml.
1 tbsp.	= 15 ml.
1 cup	= 250 ml.

VOLUME MEASUREMENTS:

1 fl. oz.	= 28.41 ml.	1 ml.	= .04 fl. oz.
1 pint	= 570 ml.	1 L.	= 1.75 pt.
1 quart	= 1.14 L.	1 L.	= .88 qt.
1 imp. gal	= 4.54 L.	1 L.	= .22 imp. gal.

LENGTH MEASUREMENTS:

1 inch	= 2.54 cm.	1 cm.	= .39 in.
1 foot	= .30 m.	1 m	= 3.28 ft.
1 yard	= .91 m.	1 m	= 1.09 yd.
1 mile	= 1.61 km.	1 km.	= .62 mi.

WEIGHT MEASUREMENTS:

1 oz.	= 28.35 gr.	1 gr.	= .04 oz.
1 lb.	= .45 kg.	1 kg.	= 2.21 lb.

TEMPERATURE EQUIVALENTS:

32 F	= 0 C	375 F	= 190 C
212 F	= 100 C	400 F	= 200 C
300 F	= 150 C	425 F	= 220 C
325 F	= 160 C	450 F	= 230 C
350 F	= 180 C		

SUBSTITUTIONS

INGREDIENTS	AMOUNTS	SUBSTITUTION
butter/margarine shortening	1 cup	7/8 cup of lard and 1/2 tsp. salt
chocolate	1 oz.	3 tbsp. cocoa and 1 tbsp. butter
egg (in custards)	1	2 egg yolks
egg (in batter)	1	1/2 tsp. baking powder
whole milk	1 cup	1/2 cup evaporated milk and 1/2 cup water
buttermilk or sour milk	1 cup	1 cup milk and 1 tbsp. vinegar
flour (all purpose)	1 cup	1 1/8 cups cake flour
flour (cake or pastry)	1 cup	7/8 cup all purpose flour
garlic	1 med. clove	1/8 tsp. garlic powder
honey	1 cup	1 cup corn syrup
ketchup	1 cup	1 cup tomato sauce, 1/2 cup sugar and 2 tbsp. vinegar
lemon	1 whole	3 - 4 tbsp. lemon juice
sugar (granulated)	1 cup	1 cup honey (use 3 tbsp. less liquid in recipe) or 1 cup brown sugar (use 1/4 cup less liquid in recipe)

BASIC GROCERY LIST ═══════

STAPLES	**DAIRY**	**VEGETABLES**
flour	milk	tomatoes
sugar	eggs	celery
baking powder	butter or	carrots
baking soda	margarine	onions
	cheese	mushrooms
	sour cream	potatoes
		lettuce

SPICES	**MEAT**	**MISC.**
salt & pepper	coldcuts	deodorant
garlic salt	hamburger	toothpaste
seasoning salt	bacon	shampoo
cinnamon	chicken	laundry soap
chili powder		hand soap
		toilet paper
		pen & paper (to write mom)

* This is just a basic list from which to start. Yours may be larger or smaller.

ACCIDENT PREVENTION ═══════

1. Carefully handle and store all toxic liquids such as cleaning compounds and pesticides.

2. Keep all toxic compounds in their original containers.

3. Read and follow all label directions on products before use.

4. Keep the phone numbers of the Poison Control Centre, Hospital, Ambulance and Police Dept., near telephone.

5. Do not use any electrical appliances such as hair dryers, curling irons or radios while taking a bath.

FIRST AID IN THE HOME ===

BURNS
FIRST DEGREE: Outer skin reddened.

SECOND DEGREE: Outer skin blistered.
(a) Remove clothing from burned area unless clothing is stuck to the burn.
(b) Hold burned area under cold running water for 10 minutes.
(c) Follow with a paste made of equal parts baking soda and water. If burn covers 10% of body or more, take victim to the hospital.
(d) Do not open blisters or contaminate with dirty materials.

THIRD DEGREE: Injured area white, dry, or charred.
(a) Hold under cool running water.
(b) Cover area with lint free cloth.
(c) Seek medical help immediately.

NOSE BLEEDS
(a) Have person tilt head forward.
(b) Pinch nostrils firmly for 10 minutes.
(c) Avoid blowing nose
(d) If bleeding continues, seek medical help.

POISONS
POISONS SWALLOWED:
Immediately call Poison Control Centre.

POISONS IN THE EYE:
(a) Flood the eye with lukewarm water poured from a large glass 2 or 3 inches from the eye.
(b) Repeat for 15 minutes.
(c) Have victim blink as much as possible while flooding eye.
(d) Do not force eye open.
(e) Seek medical treatment immediately.

POISONS ON THE SKIN:
Any toxic solutions that irritate the skin such as oven cleaner, bleach, etc.
(a) Flood skin with warm water for 10 minutes.
(b) Remove contaminated clothing and wash gently with soap and water and rinse.

INHALED POISONS:
(a) Immediately get victim to fresh air.
(b) Avoid breathing the fumes yourself.
(c) Open all doors and windows wide.
(d) If victim is not breathing, start artificial respiration.
(e) Seek medical help.

SPINE OR NECK INJURY
(a) Keep victim from moving.
(b) Send for trained medical assistance.
(c) Keep victim warm and quiet.
(d) Do not move victim unless there is a life threatening circumstance.
(e) Call for Ambulance.

CHOKING ADULT OR LARGE CHILD
(a) Deliver 4 sharp blows to the back between the
    shoulder blades.
(b) From behind, grasp the victim just below the rib cage, giving 4
    quick backward thrusts.

DEEP CUT
When blood is spurting or pulsating from a wound:
(a) Cover wound with clean cloth or dressing and apply firm
    pressure to the wound.
(b) Elevate wound if possible.
(c) If bleeding stops, continue to apply pressure for 10 minutes.
(d) Seek medical attention as soon as possible.

SMALL CUT
Blood flowing out of a small cut in a steady stream:
(a) Clean wound gently.
(b) Apply an antiseptic such as Mercurochrome.
(c) Apply clean dressing with light pressure to wound.
(d) If bleeding persists, obtain medical help.

AMPUTATION
To fingers, toes, etc.:
(a) Keep amputated part cold with ice pack.
(b) Transport amputated part with victim to the hospital.

CRUSH INJURY OR SPRAIN INJURY
To hand, fingers, ankle, toes, etc.
(a) Apply ice packs immediately to prevent swelling and bruising.
(b) Leave ice pack on 15 to 30 minutes. Make ice pack by
    putting ice cubes in a plastic bag.

FIRE PREVENTION IN THE HOME ═══════

1. Make sure you have at least one smoke detector in your home.

2. Be aware of fire escape routes.

3. Replace frayed, broken or loose wires and plugs on all electrical appliances.

4. Turn your pot handles toward the rear of your stove when cooking. This will eliminate any chance of spilling a hot pot of water on yourself.

5. Have at least one chemical fire extinguisher in the home.

6. Keep an eye on barbecues when in use.

7. Do not overload circuits with too many extension cords.

8. Never use an extension cord for your television set. This is a fire hazard. It will also impair reception.

9. Do not smoke in bed.

10. If your clothing catches on fire you should try smother flames with a blanket, rug, or coat. If that doesn't work, drop to the ground, cover face and roll. This will smother flames.

11. Do not attempt to put out a grease or electrical fire with water as this will spread the flames. Sprinkle grease fire with baking soda (It is a good idea to keep a box of baking soda handy when cooking). Use a chemical extinguisher for an electrical fire.

EMERGENCY PHONE NUMBERS

POLICE _____

FIRE _____

AMBULANCE _____

DOCTOR _____

HOSPITAL _____

MOM _____

COOKING TERMS

BAKE - to cook by dry heat, in an oven.

BARBECUE - to roast meat or other food slowly on a spit or rack over direct heat, basting with highly seasoned sauce.

BASTE - to pour liquid or melted fat over food during cooking to keep food moist and flavourful.

BEAT - to stir vigorously with spoon, egg beater or electric mixer.

BLEND - to mix two or more ingredients thoroughly.

BLANCH - to scald quickly in boiling water.

BOIL - to cook in steaming liquid in which bubbles are breaking on the surface.

BRAISE - to cook meat with a small amount of moisture in a covered saucepan or casserole.

BREAD - to coat with fine bread or cracker crumbs prior to frying or baking.

BROIL - to cook food by searing the surface with direct heat under a broiler or over hot coals.

BROWN - to briefly fry in a little hot fat until brown on the outside.

BRUSH - to spread thinly with a brush.

CHILL - to refrigerate until thoroughly cold.

CHOP - to cut in fine or coarse pieces

CLOVE OF GARLIC - one section of a garlic bulb.

COAT - to cover thoroughly with a fine film of flour, crumbs, sugar, etc.

CONDIMENT - a pungent seasoning, such as pepper, mustard, vinegar or prepared sauce.

CREAM - to soften with a wooden spoon or electric mixer until light and fluffy.

CRISP - to warm in oven until dry or brittle.

CROUTONS - small diced, dried cubes of bread.

CUT IN - to combine solid fat with dry ingredients using two knives, a fork or a pastry blender.

DASH - a quick shake of an ingredient of approximately 1/6 teaspoon.

DICE - to cut into cubes with a sharp knife on a cutting board.

DUST - to cover lightly with flour, icing sugar or other dry ingredients.

DRIPPINGS - juice and fat left in pan after roasting or frying meat, etc.

FLAKE - to break into small pieces with a fork.

FOLD IN - to combine ingredients with a gentle up and over motion without releasing air bubbles that have been beaten into the ingredients. Cut down through mixture with a broad spatula or whisk. Lift some of the mixture from the bottom to the top with each fold. Give the bowl a quarter turn with each motion until all ingredients have been blended.

FRENCH FRY - to deep fry in oil.

FROST - to cover with icing. Also, chill until frosty.

FRY - to pan fry is to cook in a small amount of fat in a frying pan.

GARNISH - to decorate with parsley, etc. around or on top of food.

GLAZE - to add lustre to a food by coating with butter, eggs, milk or syrup.

GRATE - to shred food by rubbing it over a sharp-edged grater.

GREASE - to rub and coat the inside of a baking pan with fat before pouring in batter, etc.

GRIND - to put through a food chopper; cutting or crushing.

ICE - to cover with icing.

KNEAD - to work dough with a pressing motion accompanied by folding and stretching.

LINE - to cover the bottom or sometimes sides of a pan or dish with paper or thin slices of food as directed.

MARINADE - a savory mixture of lemon juice or vinegar, seasonings, chopped or sliced vegetables and sometimes oil; may be cooked or uncooked.

MARINATE - to season and tenderize food by soaking it in a marinade.

MINCE - to grind, chop or cut into small pieces.

POACH - to cook in or above liquid at a simmer.

PREHEAT - to heat oven, frying pan, etc. to the correct cooking temperature before adding the food.

ROAST - to cook, uncovered, in the oven.

SAUTE - to brown or cook pieces of food in a small amount of fat in a frying pan, turning pieces frequently.

SCALD - to pour boiling water over vegetables, etc., draining at once or allowing to stand for a few minutes. To heat milk until bubbles form around the edge.

SIFT - to put flour or other dry ingredients through a sifter.

SIMMER - to cook just below the boiling point.

SKIM - to remove fat or oil from the surface of a liquid or sauce.

STEAM - to cook food over steam rising from a pan of boiling water or other liquid.

STEW - to cook in boiling liquid. Pot is usually covered.

THAW - to defrost a frozen substance in the refrigerator, at room temperature, in an oven or on top of the stove.

THICKEN - to add a thickening agent such as flour, egg yolks, etc.

THIN - to add liquid such as milk, water, etc.

TOSS - to mix by gently turning ingredients over and over .

WHIP - to beat rapidly with egg beater or mixer.

HELPFUL HINTS

Never buy cans that are dented. There could be a leakage that could spoil the contents.

Onion, fish or garlic odors disappear from dishes if you add a slice of lemon peel to your dishwater.

Do not wash your teapot with soap or it will lose its sweetness. Rinse with hot water only.

Never mix bleach and household ammonia together for cleaning as they will form a poisonous gas.

Place a small open box of baking soda in the fridge to absorb odors.

When cooking porridge, add a bit of margarine or butter to cooking water to help prevent sticky pans.

Use a damp cloth dipped in baking soda to remove tea or coffee stains in your coffee cups.

Clean your combs and brushes by soaking in warm water with a little ammonia added to it.

To make good tea, bring the water just to a boil. Do not let it sit boiling, as it will use up the oxygen which makes tea good.

Every month, or as needed, take everything out of your fridge and wash the inside of the fridge with warm water combined with a little dish soap and a tablespoon of baking soda or vinegar. You will have a clean and fresh-smelling fridge.

For shiny glassware, add a little vinegar to the rinse water before wiping dry.

A bowl of vinegar placed in a smoky or stuffy room will absorb the tobacco smoke and keep the air fresh.

If you don't have a rolling pin, use a bottle or jar to crush crackers or bread crumbs. Place crumbs in plastic bag to avoid a mess when crushing.

Use up stale bread by drying bread slices in 300 degree oven for 20 minutes. Crush for crumbs when required.

If you like soft cookies, add a piece of bread to the cookie jar. It will keep cookies soft for 2 - 3 days.

When cooking pasta, add about 1 tbsp. vegetable oil to the water to keep pasta from sticking together.

Garlic smells won't linger on your fingers if you pound the cloves between two pieces of waxed paper.

FOOD STORAGE

Store up to 1 year;
Canned foods: fruits, vegetables, juices, meats and fish. Dried foods, packaged desserts, gelatins, all pasta noodles, rice, tapioca, barley, dried peas, beans, sugars, syrups, flour, cornstarch.

Store up to 6 months;
Frozen fruits, vegetables, juices, roasts, poultry (at 0 degrees F), shortening, salad oil (in refrigerator), packaged cereals, crackers, nuts (in refrigerator or freezer), dried fruits (in covered containers), spices, condiments, baking powder and soda.

Store up to 2 months;
Butter, margarine (in refrigerator).

Store up to 1 month;
Ice cream, cookies, potatoes, onions and carrots.

Store up to 1 week;
Fresh milk, cream, cottage cheese, eggs, breads and cakes.

Use as soon as possible;
Ground meat, fresh poultry, fish, chops, variety meats, fresh fruits and vegetables.

THIS IS THE WAY
WE WASH OUR CLOTHES ═══════

Remember when ......

All that dirty laundry,
You'd left lying on the floor,
Was picked up, washed and ironed
And folded for your drawer?

Well, now the destiny of your clothing depends solely upon your laundering skills. However, some organization and a little know-how should make you a super launderer in no time. So let's get down to the nitty gritty:

1. Make sure you separate items that give off lint (such as towels, sweaters) from those that attract lint (knits, permanent press). In other words, don't wash your black cords with an orange towel or you'll be picking orange fuzz off your pants from now until Halloween!

2. Most garments have labels containing symbols which tell you how to wash, dry, iron and/or dry clean the item. Be sure to read and follow these instructions carefully.

3. Laundry detergents should be added to the wash water before you add your clothes. If using bleach, do the same. **Never** add bleach undiluted to a load already in. Read manufacturer's directions for use.

4. Zip all zippers, hook all hooks (to prevent snags in clothing). Make sure all pockets are empty and knits are turned inside out (so they won't catch lint), before washing.

5. Don't overload your washer. Tightly-packed clothes can't circulate freely and won't get as clean as they should.

6. Will the colour run? If you are uncertain, dip a portion of the item in water. Make sure it's the same temperature as you intend to use for washing. Let the fabric sit for several minutes, then squeeze it. If the colour runs, wash the garment separately in cold water, or wash it with fabrics of similar colour.

7. When drying clothes, don't overdo it! Remove items from dryer when they're dry, but not bone-dry. Shake out articles, then fold or hang immediately.

8. If the clothing has wrinkles, but you don't have an iron, hang the item in a steamy bathroom while you have a shower.

9. Don't leave damp clothes in your laundry basket, dryer or clothes hamper, as this could cause mildew to form on them.

10. If you don't have a laundry basket, use a large clena plastic garbage bag to transport your laundry to and from the laundromat.

NOTE: Many detergent boxes list an address to write for laundry tips. Go for it! It's well worth the price of a stamp.

By the way, while you're waiting for your laundry to wash or dry, why not catch up on your letter writing back home?

REMOVING TOUGH STAINS
(This should be done prior to laundering)

Invest in a good spray laundry cleaner. Test any stain remover on the inside seam or other inconspicuous spot of the garment to make sure it doesn't affect the colour.

Blood:
Soak garment in cold water for up to one hour. (Never use hot water). Spray with laundry cleaner then wash.

Candle Wax:
Rub with ice. Scrape off wax with a dull knife. Place the spot between two pieces of blotting or tissue paper and press with warm iron. Replace paper often to absorb more wax. Spray with cleaner then wash.

Chocolate:
Sponge with warm water immediately. Spray with cleaner then wash.

Fruit, Wine or Soft Drinks:
Soak fresh stains immediately in cool water. Wash in hottest water safe for the fabric.

Gum:
Rub with ice until the gum hardens. If a stain remains after scraping off gum, spray with cleaner before washing.

Ink:
Some ink stains may be removed with rubbing alcohol or hairspray!

Lipstick:
Place stain face-down on paper towels and sponge with rubbing alcohol, replacing the paper towel underneath often so that more of the colour will be removed.

Perspiration:
Apply vinegar to stain. Soak in warm water using a presoak cleaner.

Ring around the collar? Apply shampoo and let it soak about 2 - 3 minutes before washing.

NOTE: Never dry silky polyesters (such as some blouses or dresses) in a dryer as they will pick up stains from the film of fabric softeners used in previous loads. If you do forget about this tip and end up with a stained garment, spray it with a good laundry spray cleaner, wash again and hang to dry.

LAUNDRY SORTING

Whites:
These include white or plain pastel sheets, underwear, shirts, towels, handkerchiefs and white socks. Wash in hot water (and bleach, if really dirty) for 10 - 15 minutes.

Light Colours:
Shirts, blouses, dresses, printed sheets, towels, cotton underwear. Wash in warm water 8 - 10 minutes. Rinse in cold.

Bright and Deep Colours:
T-shirts, shirts, dresses, knits, pantyhose, etc. To prevent shrinking and fading, wash in cold water 8 - 10 minutes. Rinse in cold as well.

Darks:
Jeans, cords, dark socks, etc. Wash in warm water 8 -10 minutes. Rinse in cold.

Delicates:
Lace-trimmed items, lingerie, pantyhose or anything sheer. Wash in warm water 5 - 8 minutes. Rinse in cold.

Woollens:
Washable sweaters, scarves, etc. Always wash delicate woollens by hand in cool or cold water. No need to spend lots on special soap — use shampoo or gentle dishwashing (not dishwasher) detergent. Soak garments 2 - 3 minutes. Squeeze gently by hand until clean (do not rub or twist). Rinse in cold water, and roll in a towel to remove moisture. Don't wring the garment. Reshape it, and dry in a flat spot away from direct heat.

LAUNDRY SYMBOLS

RED	AMBER	GREEN
Stop	Be careful	Go ahead

Machine washable
in warm water.

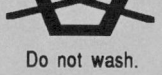

Do not wash.

Machine washable in
lukewarm water.

Machine washable
in hot water.

Hand washable in
lukewarm water.

Use chlorine
bleach as directed.

Do not bleach.

Tumble dry low.

Tumble dry medium-high.

Hang to dry soaking-wet.

Dry flat.

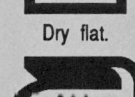

Iron medium.

Hang to dry.

Do not Iron.

Iron low.

Iron high.

Do not dry clean.

Dry clean low.

Dry clean.

BREAKFASTS

SOFT BOILED EGG

TEMP: high
COOKING TIME: 4 - 5 minutes
MAKES: 1 egg

DIRECTIONS:
1. Bring water to a boil in pot.
2. Carefully place egg in boiling water.
3. Boil for 4 - 5 minutes.
4. Immediately run cold water over egg to stop cooking process.

NOTE: Serve with toast and bacon.

HARD BOILED EGG

TEMP: high
COOKING TIME: 15 - 17 minutes
MAKES: 1 egg

DIRECTIONS:
1. Place egg in pot of cold water (just enough to cover the egg).
2. When water comes to a boil, cook for another 10 minutes.
3. Put egg in cold water for about 2 minutes, then peel.

SCRAMBLED EGGS

TEMP: medium - high
COOKING TIME: 5 minutes
PREPARATION TIME: 5 minutes
MAKES: 1 serving

INGREDIENTS:
2 eggs
2 tbsp. milk

1 tbsp. butter
salt and pepper to taste

DIRECTIONS:
1. Beat eggs, milk, salt and pepper.
2. Melt butter in small skillet.
3. Pour egg mixture into skillet.
4. Cook, stirring continuously until mixture thickens.

NOTE: Do not overcook unless you like rubber eggs.

QUICK OVEN OMELETTE ════════

TEMP: 350 degrees
COOKING TIME: 40 minutes
PREPARATION TIME: 15 minutes
MAKES: 4 - 6 servings

INGREDIENTS:
5 large eggs
1 1/4 cups milk
1 1/2 cups colby or cheddar cheese, grated
1/4 lb. cooked ham, cut in thin strips
1/4 cup green onion, finely chopped
1/4 tsp. salt
1 tbsp. flour

DIRECTIONS:
1. Butter 9" round baking pan or pie plate.
2. Beat eggs until blended, stir in milk.
3. Combine cheese, ham, onion, and salt. Add flour and toss lightly
4. Stir into egg mixture and pour into buttered dish.
5. Bake at 350 degrees for 35 - 40 minutes or until set.
6. Spoon from dish to serve.

RICE AND RAISIN KASHA ════════

TEMP: medium
COOKING TIME: 30 - 45 minutes
PREPARATION TIME: 5 minutes
MAKES: 2 - 3 servings

INGREDIENTS:
3 cups milk   1/2 tsp. salt
1/2 cup rice   2 tbsp. butter or margarine
1/2 cup raisins

DIRECTIONS:
1. Pour milk into a pot, add salt and bring to a boil.
2. Reduce heat and add rice. Cover and cook about 25 minutes, stirring often.
3. Wash raisins. Add to mixture and cook another 5 - 10 minutes.
4. Stir in butter and sprinkle with brown sugar, if desired.

NOTE: More milk may be added if Kasha is too thick.

HINT: To prevent milk from scorching, rinse pot with cold water before

BASIC OMELETTE ═══════════

TEMP: medium - high
COOKING TIME: 5 minutes
PREPARATION TIME: 2 minutes
MAKES: 1 serving

INGREDIENTS:
2 eggs
1 tsp. water
 salt and pepper to taste
1 tsp. butter

DIRECTIONS:
1. Beat eggs and add water, salt and pepper.
2   Melt butter in 8" skillet.
3. Add egg mixture to skillet when butter is melted.
4. While cooking, gently lift edges so uncooked portion of egg
   mixture flows underneath cooked portion. Repeat procedure until
   egg is set.
5. Fold in half and serve immediately.

NOTE: With omelettes, anything goes! Try mushrooms, green
 pepper, chunks of bacon or other meat, onion, cheese or anything
else you have in the fridge. These may be added when eggs are
partially set.

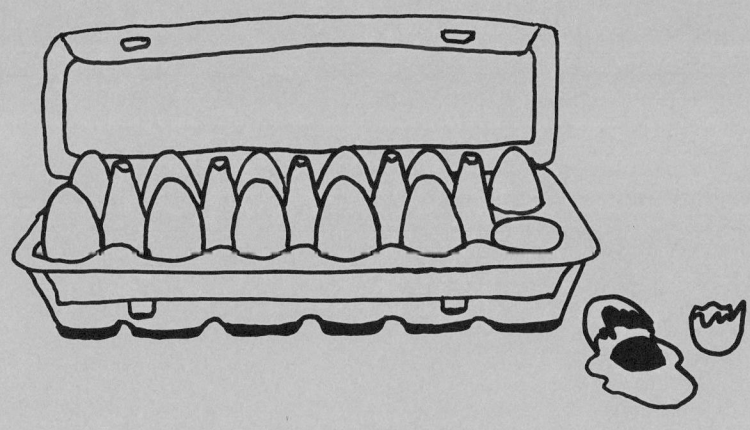

POACHED EGG

TEMP: high
COOKING TIME: 2 - 3 minutes
MAKES: 1 serving

INGREDIENTS:

1 egg
1 tbsp. white vinegar

1/8 tsp. salt
1/8 tsp. pepper

DIRECTIONS:
1. In a 3-quart saucepan, pour water to depth of 3". Add vinegar and bring to a boil.
2. Reduce heat to simmer.
3. Break egg in shallow dish.
4. Stir water until it swirls. Gently slip in egg into swirling water.
5. Cook until egg is set as desired and remove egg with slotted spoon.
6. Season to taste and serve on toast.

NOTE: Vinegar helps to set egg whites.

PANCAKES

TEMP: medium to high
COOKING TIME: approximately 5 minutes
PREPARATION TIME: 10 minutes
MAKES: 6 pancakes

INGREDIENTS:

1 1/2 cups flour
3 tsp. baking powder
1 tbsp. sugar
1/2 tsp. salt

1 3/4 cups milk
2 tbsp. oil
butter or margarine
1 egg, beaten

OPTIONAL: Add 1/2 a cup of the following: blueberries, chopped apple or well-drained crushed pineapple.

DIRECTIONS:
1. Mix beaten egg with milk and oil.
2 Combine flour, baking powder, salt and sugar.
3. Mix liquid ingredients with dry ingredients.
4. Grease pan with butter or margarine.
5. Pour about 1/2 cup of batter per pancake into pan and cook until they start to bubble then flip and cook until golden brown.

FRENCH TOAST

TEMP: medium - high
COOKING TIME: 5 - 10 minutes
PREPARATION TIME: 5 minutes
MAKES: 4 slices

INGREDIENTS:
2 eggs
1/4 cup milk
2 tsp. butter
4 slices bread
jam or syrup

OPTIONAL: 1/2 tsp. cinnamon.

DIRECTIONS:
1. Beat eggs and milk in bowl.
2. Pour mixture into a shallow pan (eg. tin pie plate).
3. Melt butter in frying pan.
4. Dip bread in egg mixture and put in frying pan.
5. Sprinkle with cinnamon.
6. When slightly browned, flip slices and cook until golden brown.
7. Serve with syrup.

CINNAMON TOAST

TEMP: broil
COOKING TIME: 1 - 2 minutes
PREPARATION TIME: 10 minutes
MAKES: 2 servings

INGREDIENTS:

4 slices bread
2 tbsp. butter or margarine

1/4 cup brown sugar
2 tsp. cinnamon

DIRECTIONS:
1. Mix butter, brown sugar and cinnamon.
2. Toast bread.
3. Spread butter mixture over hot toast.
4. Place under broiler until bubbly.

VARIATIONS:
1. Mix butter, brown sugar, a dash of nutmeg and cinnamon. Spread on bread and toast under broiler.
2. Mix 2 tsp. cinnamon and 5 tbsp. icing sugar. Put into an old salt shaker and shake over freshly buttered toast.

BUTTERMILK PANCAKES

TEMP: medium (electric frying pan 400 degrees)
COOKING TIME: 5-10 minutes
PREPARATION TIME: 10 minutes
MAKES: 6 pancakes

INGREDIENTS:

1 egg, beaten
1 cup buttermilk
1 tsp. sugar
1/2 tsp. salt

1 tsp. baking powder
1/2 tsp. baking soda
1 tbsp. butter or oil
1 cup flour

DIRECTIONS:
1. Preheat frying pan.
2. Mix egg and buttermilk together.
3. Add all dry ingredients and stir well.
4. Melt butter and add to mixture.
5. Grease pan with butter or cooking oil.
6. Pour about 1/2 cup of batter per pancake into frying pan.
7. Flip pancakes when they start to bubble.

BREADS and SANDWICHES ===

SANDWICH FILLINGS

PREPARATION TIME: 10 minutes
MAKES: 2 servings

CHICKEN FILLING

INGREDIENTS:
1/3 cup cooked chicken, finely chopped
2 tsp. onion, finely chopped
2 tsp. green pepper, finely chopped
dash of curry powder or 1/2 tsp. lemon juice
1 1/3 tbsp. mayonnaise

HAM FILLING

INGREDIENTS:
1/3 cup cooked ham, chopped
1 1/3 tbsp. sweet pickle, chopped
dash of Tabasco sauce
1/4 tsp. prepared mustard
2 tsp. mayonnaise

CHEESE FILLING

INGREDIENTS:
1/2 cup cheddar cheese, grated
2 tbsp. celery, finely chopped
1 tsp. green onion chopped
dash of Tabasco sauce
2 tbsp. mayonnaise

OPTIONAL: 1 tbsp. chopped pimento.

DIRECTIONS:
For all above fillings, mix the ingredients listed in a bowl, then spread
on bread or stuff in pita bread.

DEVILLED EGG FILLING ════════════

COOKING TIME: 10 minutes
PREPARATION TIME: 10 minutes
MAKES: 2 sandwich fillings

INGREDIENTS:
2 eggs (hard boiled)
1 tbsp. onion, chopped
3 tbsp. mayonnaise
salt to taste

OPTIONAL: 1/2 cup shredded lettuce, 1/4 cup chopped celery,
1 tbsp. relish, garlic salt to taste, seasoning salt to taste, 1 tbsp. finely
chopped pickles and 2 tbsp. grated cheese.

DIRECTIONS:
1. Run cold water over hard boiled eggs for easy peeling.
2. Mash eggs with a fork.
3. Add dry ingredients.

EGG LUNCH ════════════

TEMP: medium
COOKING TIME: 10 minutes
PREPARATION TIME: 10 minutes
MAKES: 4 servings

INGREDIENTS:
10 oz. can mushroom soup
1/4 cup water
3 hard boiled eggs, chopped
4 slices bread, toasted

OPTIONAL: 1/4 cup peas, 1/4 cup drained mushrooms or chicken
soup instead of mushroom soup.

DIRECTIONS:
1. Combine soup, water and eggs.
2. Mix lightly and heat on medium.
3. Serve on buttered toast.

NOTE: May be served on cooked rice instead of toast and then
sprinkled with grated cheese.

EGG BURGER

TEMP: medium
COOKING TIME: 5 minutes
PREPARATION TIME: 5 minutes
MAKES: 1 burger

INGREDIENTS:

1 tsp. butter
1 egg
1/8 tsp. salt
1/8 tsp. pepper
1 hamburger bun
1 slice cheddar cheese

2 - 3 mushrooms, sliced
1 slice tomato
leaf of lettuce
1 slice onion
mayonnaise

DIRECTIONS:
1. Split and toast bun. Spread with butter, mayonnaise, etc.
2. Melt butter in pan on medium heat.
3. Saute mushrooms about 3 minutes.
4. Top with cheese and heat until cheese melts.
5. Put mushroom/cheese mixture on bun.
6. Fry egg in same pan.
7. Top mushroom/cheese mixture with egg.
8. Add tomato, lettuce and onion to egg burger and serve.

GRILLED CHEESE SANDWICH

TEMP: medium
COOKING TIME: 2 minutes each side
PREPARATION TIME: 10 minutes
MAKES: 2 sandwiches

INGREDIENTS:
4 slices of bread
butter or margarine
2 slices cheese

DIRECTIONS:
1. Place slice of cheese between bread.
2. Place frying pan on medium heat.
3. Spread butter on outsides of sandwiches.
4. Place in frying pan and cook until golden brown on each side.

NOTES: Many variations may be tried with this recipe. Try it with a slice of ham, a tomato, onions or cooked bacon.

TUNA IN A PITA POCKET

PREPARATION TIME: 10 minutes
MAKES : 2 servings

INGREDIENTS:
6 1/2 oz. can tuna, drained
3 tbsp. green onion, chopped
1/2 cup carrots, grated
1 apple, cored and finely chopped
4 tsp. mayonnaise
1 tsp. mustard
2 pita bread
leafy lettuce

OPTIONAL: 1/2 cup grated zucchini, 1/4 cup finely chopped celery,
1 tsp. poppy seeds.

DIRECTIONS:
1. Combine tuna, apple, zucchini, carrots and onion.
2. Combine mayonnaise, mustard and poppy seeds.
3. Toss the two mixtures together lightly.
4. Cut pita bread in half and open to form pocket.
5. Butter pita if desired. Line pocket with lettuce and fill with tuna
   mixture.

NOTE: You may want to garnish with parsley and radishes. Filling
may also be used for basic sandwich.

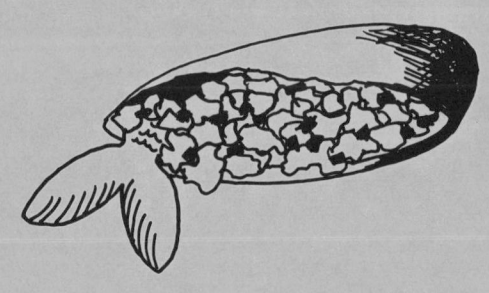

BROILED TUNA SANDWICH

TEMP: broil
COOKING TIME: 3 minutes
PREPARATION TIME: 10 - 15 minutes
MAKES: 6 buns

INGREDIENTS:
6 1/2 oz. can tuna, drained
2 eggs, hard boiled and chopped
1 green onion, chopped
1/2 cup celery, chopped
salt and pepper to taste

3 burger buns, cut in half
3 tbsp. butter
3/4 cup cheese, grated
3 tbsp. mayonnaise

OPTIONAL: 1 tbsp. minced parsley and alfalfa sprouts.

DIRECTIONS:
1. Turn on oven and place rack on highest position.
2. Put first five ingredients in mixing bowl and mix thoroughly.
3. Add mayonnaise so mixture will spread easily.
4. Spread buns with soft butter and broil until golden brown .
5. Spread with tuna/egg mixture.
6. Sprinkle with alfalfa sprouts.
7. Top with grated cheese.
8. Broil until cheese melts. Serve hot.

GARLIC BREAD

TEMP: broil
COOKING TIME: 10 minutes
PREPARATION TIME: 5 minutes
MAKES: 4 servings

INGREDIENTS:
8 slices bread or any bread bun
1/2 cup butter or margarine
1/2 tsp. garlic salt or garlic powder

OPTIONAL: Parmesan cheese may be added after butter.

DIRECTIONS:
1. Slice bread 3/4" thick.
2. Soften butter.
3. Stir in garlic powder.
4. Spread on bread generously.
5. Place on baking sheet and broil until golden brown.

TV TUNA SPECIAL

TEMP: 350 degrees
COOKING TIME: 20 minutes
PREPARATION TIME: 10 minutes
MAKES: 6 servings

INGREDIENTS:

7 oz. can flaked tuna
1 cup cheddar cheese, grated
2 tbsp. onion, finely chopped

2 tbsp. prepared mustard
6 hot dog buns

OPTIONAL: 2 tbsp. finely chopped sweet pickles.

DIRECTIONS:
1. Drain tuna.
2. Mix all ingredients together (except buns).
3. Cut hot dog buns lengthwise almost through and fill each with fish mixture.
4. Wrap each roll in aluminum foil and heat in oven for 20 minutes.

DENVER SANDWICH

TEMP: medium
COOKING TIME: 15 minutes
PREPARATION TIME: 15 minutes
MAKES: 4 servings

INGREDIENTS:

1 1/2 cups cooked ham, cubed
1/4 cup margarine
6 eggs
1 med. onion, cut in eighths

1 medium green pepper
1/2 tsp. salt
1/4 tsp. pepper
8 slices bread

OPTIONAL: Add any cubed cold cuts, celery or fresh cubed tomato before egg.

DIRECTIONS:
1. Preheat frying pan.
2. Chop ham, onion, and green pepper finely.
3. Saute in margarine about 5 minutes.
4. Beat eggs, salt and pepper.
5. Pour over ham mixture, cover pan and cook until firm. (This may also be stirred like scrambled eggs.)
6. Spread filling on bread to make sandwiches.

TACOS

TEMP: low - medium
COOKING TIME: 20 minutes
PREPARATION TIME: 15 minutes
MAKES: 4 servings

INGREDIENTS:
1 lb. ground beef
3/4 cup onion, chopped
1/2 cup green pepper, chopped
1 clove garlic, crushed
8 oz. can tomato sauce
1 tsp. chili powder
1 tsp. salt
1/4 tsp. black pepper
12 taco shells
1/3 cup tomatoes, chopped
1 cup lettuce, chopped
1 cup cheese, grated

OPTIONAL: 1/8 tsp. garlic powder instead of clove, bottled taco sauce for topping, monterey jack cheese.

DIRECTIONS:
1. Saute beef, onion, green pepper and garlic until beef is browned and onion is tender.
2. Spoon off any excess fat.
3. Stir in tomato sauce, chili powder, salt and pepper.
4. Cook, on low heat, uncovered until thickened, about 10 -15 minutes.
5. Spoon meat mixture into taco shells and top with some tomato, lettuce and cheese.
6. Sprinkle with taco sauce and serve.

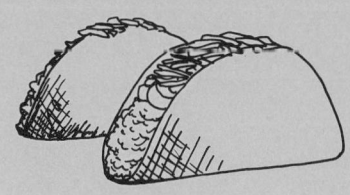

TACO CHEESE MELT

TEMP: 350 degrees
COOKING TIME: 10 minutes
PREPARATION TIME: 5 minutes
MAKES: 5 servings

INGREDIENTS:
1 cup cheese, grated (any kind)
3 cups taco chips

DIRECTIONS:
1. Spread tacos in one layer on cookie sheet.
2. Sprinkle cheese over top.
3. Bake at 350 degrees until cheese has melted (10 minutes).
4. Great snack when watching TV or doing homework.

PIZZA BUNS

TEMP: broil
COOKING TIME: 5 minutes
PREPARATION TIME: 10 - 15 minutes
MAKES: 12 buns

INGREDIENTS:
7 oz. can tomato paste
1/4 cup oil
2 cups mozzarella cheese, grated
1 medium onion, chopped fine
1/4 tsp. garlic salt
1/4 tsp. pepper
1/4 tsp. salt
6 hamburger buns

OPTIONAL: Cheddar cheese in place of mozzarella. 1/2 cup green pepper, mushrooms or ham may be added.

DIRECTIONS:
1. Place oven rack in middle position. Preheat broiler.
2. Combine tomato paste, oil, cheese, onion, garlic, salt and pepper.
3. Cut buns in half and spread with tomato mixture.
4. Cheese may be sprinkled on top.
5. Place on ungreased cookie sheet in oven and broil until bubbly (approximately 2 minutes.)

NOTE: 3/4 cup ketchup or spaghetti sauce can be substituted for the tomato paste.

SLOPPY JOES ===

TEMP: 300 degrees
COOKING TIME: 20 minutes
PREPARATION TIME: 10 minutes
MAKES: 4 - 6 servings

INGREDIENTS:

1 lb. ground beef
1/2 cup onions, chopped
1/2 cup celery, chopped
1 tbsp. Worcestershire sauce
1 cup (approximately) cheese, grated

10 oz. can tomato soup
1 tsp. salt
1 tbsp. mustard
4 - 6 mini French loaves
1 tbsp. oil

DIRECTIONS:
1. Brown ground beef, onions and celery in oil.
2. Add remaining ingredients.
3. Simmer 20 minutes.
4. Slice mini French loaves horizontally and spoon mix over loaves.
5. Sprinkle each with grated cheddar cheese.
6. Wrap each in foil.
7. Bake at 300 degrees for 10 minutes.

NOTE: The sauce may be used over your favorite pasta or rice dish.

SOUR MILK BISCUITS ===

TEMP: 450 degrees
COOKING TIME: 10 minutes
PREPARATION TIME: 5 minutes
MAKES: 12 biscuits

INGREDIENTS:

2 cups flour
1 tsp. baking powder
1/2 tsp. baking soda

1 tsp. salt
1/4 cup soft margarine
1 cup buttermilk

DIRECTIONS:
1. Sift together flour, baking powder, baking soda and salt.
2. Cut in margarine. Add buttermilk then mix.
3. Turn out on floured surface.
4. Knead 20 times. Roll out to 1/2" thick.
5. Cut into 12 pieces.
6. Bake on cookie sheet in 450 degree oven for 10 minutes.

GRILLED REUBEN SANDWICH ≡≡≡

TEMP: medium
COOKING TIME: 5 minutes
PREPARATION TIME: 5 minutes
MAKES: 1 sandwich

INGREDIENTS:
2 slices rye bread
Thousand Islands dressing
1 slice Danish cheese

1 tbsp. sauerkraut
1 slice corned beef
butter

OPTIONAL: Replace the above with pumpernickel bread, Swiss cheese or pastrami.

DIRECTIONS:
1. Spread one side of bread with Thousand Islands dressing.
2. Add sauerkraut, corned beef and cheese. Cover with another slice of bread.
3. Melt butter in skillet and brown sandwich lightly on both sides.
4. Serve with dill pickles or olives.

OPEN FACE SANDWICH ≡≡≡

TEMP: broil
COOKING TIME: 5 minutes
PREPARATION TIME: 10 minutes
MAKES: 4 servings

INGREDIENTS:
4 English muffins
1 tbsp. margarine
8 slices salami
1/2 cup lettuce, chopped

1/2 small onion
1 medium tomato
1/8 tsp. basil
4 slices cheese

DIRECTIONS:
1. Wash vegetables.
2. Preheat broiler and toast muffins under broiler, then butter them.
3. Slice and quarter salami, then chop lettuce, slice tomatoes and dice onions.
4. Layer vegetables and salami on top of muffin, sprinkle with basil. Top each sandwich with slice of cheese. Broil until cheese melts and is slightly brown.

SOUPS
and SALADS ━━

GREEN SALAD

1. Use a variety of raw vegetables in combinations of two or more, to make a salad.
2. All salad ingredients should be crisp and well chilled.
3. Do not buy lettuce which has speckles of "rust" on its leaves, as the whole head will usually be affected in this way.
4. Wash vegetables in cold water. Gently shake off excess water and drain well on a clean tea towel.
5. Separate lettuce, endive or spinach into leaves, and discard any which are bruised or wilted.
6. Tear, do not cut, lettuce into bite-size pieces and put into a salad bowl.
7. Add one or more combinations of any of the following. These are only suggestions, so you can let your imagination take over:

tomatoes	carrots
radish	cauliflowerettes
cucumbers	green or red onion
red cabbage	green or red pepper
celery	raw mushrooms

8. Toss vegetables gently with forks.
9. Chill in refrigerator until ready to serve. Add your choice of dressing when ready to eat.

NOTE: Serve with French dressing (see sauces) if desired, hard rolls or French bread. Vary these with garlic butter or a sprinkle of garlic salt.

KWAS (Cold Cucumber Soup)

PREPARATION TIME: 5 - 10 minutes
MAKES: 4 servings

INGREDIENTS:
4 cups cold water
2 cucumbers 6" - 8" long
1/4 cup green onions, chopped

4 tbsp. lemon juice
1 tsp. salt

OPTIONAL: 1/4 cup fresh dill or 2 tsp. dried dill weed.

DIRECTIONS:
1. Finely grate cucumbers.
2. Add onion, lemon juice, water and salt.
3. Sprinkle dill on top.
4. A few ice cubes may be added just before serving.

NOTE: Serve with potatoes and other vegetables.

DUMPLING SOUP

TEMP: medium
COOKING TIME: 15 minutes
PREPARATION TIME: 20 minutes
MAKES: 4 servings

INGREDIENTS:
1 small onion
3 tbsp. butter
1 qt. water
1/2 tsp. salt
2 medium potatoes, cubed

DOUGH:
1 egg, beaten
1/2 cup milk
1/2 tsp. salt
1 cup flour
1/2 tsp. baking
        powder

DIRECTIONS:
1. Bring water to a boil in a Dutch oven or a large pot.
2. Peel and cube potatoes.
3. Add salt and potatoes to boiling water.
4. Boil until potatoes are tender (approximately 5 minutes).
5. Add beaten egg to milk. Then add remaining salt, flour,
   and baking powder to mixture and stir well.
6. Drop dough by the teaspoonful into boiling water.
7. Boil until dough rises to surface (approximately 5 minutes).
8. Melt butter in small frying pan, add chopped onion,
   then saute for 3 minutes.
9. Add to soup, stir and serve.

CHINESE NOODLE SOUP

TEMP: medium
COOKING TIME: 25 minutes
PREPARATION TIME: 15 minutes
MAKES: 2 servings

INGREDIENTS:
85 gr. package Chinese noodles 1/4 cup onion, chopped
1/4 cup carrot, chopped   approximately 4 cups water
1/4 cup celery, chopped

DIRECTIONS:
1. Boil 4 cups water and add chopped vegetables. Continue to boil another 15 minutes.
2. Remove seasoning pouch from noodle package.
3. Crumble noodles and add to boiling vegetables.
4. Cook about 5 minutes then add seasoning .
5. Simmer about 10 minutes.

CHILLED BEAN SALAD

PREPARATION TIME: 10 minutes
MAKES: 6 - 8 servings

INGRDIENTS:
2 - 14 oz. cans green beans
14 oz. can yellow beans
1 green or red pepper, chopped
10 cherry tomatoes or 2 tomatoes, chopped

DRESSING:
2 tbsp. vegetable oil   1 tsp. parsley, chopped
2 tbsp. water   1 clove garlic, crushed
2 tbsp. vinegar   1/2 tsp. dill
1/2 tsp. dry mustard   1/4 tsp. oregano
1 tsp. basil leaves

OPTIONAL: 1/4 tsp. garlic powder instead of garlic clove.

DIRECTIONS:
1. Combine dressing ingredients and set aside.
2. Drain beans and combine with pepper and tomato.
3. Pour dressing into bean mixture and combine gently.
4. Chill until serving time or overnight, stirring occasionally.

POTATO SALAD

PREPARATION TIME: 1 hour
MAKES: 4 - 6 servings

INGREDIENTS:
6 medium potatoes
6 eggs, hard boiled
1/2 cup onion, chopped
1/4 cup celery, chopped
salt and pepper to taste

OPTIONAL: 3 chopped green onions, 1/4 cup chopped green
pepper, 1/4 cup grated carrot.

DIRECTIONS:
1. Boil potatoes in skins until tender when pierced with a fork, 30
   minutes. Cool. (Or use left-over potatoes.)
2. Boil eggs, drain and cool.
3. Peel potatoes and eggs and chop into cubes.
4. Mix all ingredients and add salt and pepper to taste.
5. Add dressing when ready to serve.

NOTE: Run cold water over boiled eggs for easier peeling.

DRESSING INGREDIENTS:
1/2 cup mayonnaise or salad dressing
1/4 cup sour cream
1 tsp. prepared mustard
salt and pepper to taste

OPTIONAL: 1/2 tsp. garlic salt, 1/2 tsp. fresh dill.

DIRECTIONS: Combine all dressing ingredients together and mix
into potato mixture. If ingredients for dressing are not available use
mayonnaise only.

NOTE: Plain yogurt can be substituted for sour cream.   If dressing is
too thick dilute with a little milk or oil.

WARNING: Do not let potato salad stand unrefrigerated for longer
than one hour.

FRUIT SALAD

PREPARATION TIME: 10 minutes
MAKES: 4 servings

INGREDIENTS:
1 cup miniature marshmallows
1 cup mandarin oranges, drained
1 cup pineapple chunks, drained
1 cup sour cream

OPTIONAL: 1 cup apples, bananas, grapes, peaches, melon or any fruit.

DIRECTIONS:
1. Combine the first 3 ingredients and any options.
2. Stir in sour cream.

JELLO FRUIT SALAD

PREPARATION TIME: 10 minutes
MAKES: 4 servings

INGREDIENTS:
130 gr. box Jello (any flavour)
1 medium banana
1 orange
1 apple
14 oz. can fruit cocktail mix
1 cup whipped topping or ice cream

OPTIONAL: Other fruits may be added.

DIRECTIONS:
1. Mix Jello according to directions.
2. Chop all fruit and add to drained fruit cocktail.
3. Add fruit mixture to Jello and let stand for 4 hours.
4. Place in serving dishes and top with whipped topping or ice cream.

NO - WILT MACARONI SALAD

TEMP: medium - high
PREPARATION TIME: 30 minutes
MAKES: 4 - 6 servings

INGREDIENTS:
2 cups broccoli pieces
1 cup carrots, sliced
1 cup peas, cooked
2 cups fresh mushrooms
1 green or red pepper
1 1/2 cups macaroni, cooked
3 eggs, hard boiled
2/3 cup Italian dressing
1 clove garlic, crushed
1/4 tsp. salt
1/4 tsp. pepper

OPTIONAL: 3 - 4 slices cooked, crumbled bacon.

DIRECTIONS:
1. Cook broccoli and carrots approximately 4 minutes.
2. Boil sliced mushrooms 5 - 10 minutes and drain.
3. Chop pepper and eggs.
4. Cook macaroni according to package directions.
5. Combine all ingredients.
6. Chill 6 hours or overnight.
7. Stir occasionally to coat all ingredients evenly with dressing.

TUNA CRUNCH SALAD

PREPARATION TIME: 20 minutes
MAKES: 4 servings

INGREDIENTS:
7 oz. can tuna, drained
2 cups carrots, grated
1/2 cup celery, sliced
1/4 cup onion, finely chopped
6 tbsp. mayonnaise (or to taste)
4 oz. can shoestring potatoes or 2 cups crushed potato chips
crisp lettuce

DIRECTIONS:
1. Separate tuna into chunks.
2. Place in a large bowl.
3. Add carrots, celery, onion, and mayonnaise and mix gently.
4. Cover and chill.
5. Just before serving, fold in potatoes.
6. Arrange in lettuce-lined bowl, garnish with parsley and carrot curls if desired.

ORANGE SALAD

PREPARATION TIME: 10 minutes
MAKES: 6 servings

INGREDIENTS:
2 cups creamed cottage cheese
85 gr. package orange jelly powder
14 oz. can crushed pineapple
2 cups Cool Whip or 1 package Dream Whip
10 oz. can mandarin oranges, drained

DIRECTIONS:
1. Combine cottage cheese and dry jelly powder and stir well.
2. Add undrained pineapple.
3. Fold in Cool Whip or Dream Whip.
4. Add drained oranges.

NOTE: Can be eaten immediately or kept for about three days in the fridge.

EASY GREEK TOMATO SALAD ═══════

PREPARATION TIME: 10 minutes
MAKES: 4 - 5 servings

INGREDIENTS:

5 ripe tomatoes
1 cup feta cheese
12 black olives, pitted
2 tbsp. olive oil or vegetable oil

2 tbsp. wine vinegar
1 tsp. dried basil
1/2 tsp. salt
1/4 tsp. pepper

DIRECTIONS:
1. Wash tomatoes
2. Cut into 1" cubes or wedges, and arrange on a large plate.
3. Crumble the feta cheese over the tomatoes.
4. Decorate with black olives.
5. Sprinkle the oil, vinegar, basil, salt and pepper evenly over the salad.
6. Serve at once.

LAYERED GREEN SALAD ═══════

PREPARATION TIME: 15 minutes
MAKES: 4 servings

INGREDIENTS:

1/2 head of green lettuce, chopped
1/2 cup peas, cooked
1/2 cup celery, chopped
3 green onions, chopped
7 oz. can water chestnuts, sliced
3/4 cup mayonnaise
1 cup Swiss cheese, grated

DIRECTIONS:
1. Layer the above ingredients in the order listed and serve.

VEGETABLES
and
VEGETARIAN
DISHES

BOILING VEGETABLES ====

Wash all vegetables before cooking. Use about 1/2" water for most vegetables or 1" for potatoes and vegetables that require a longer cooking time. Bring water to a boil on high heat, add 1/8 teaspoon salt and add prepared vegetables. Cover with lid and turn heat down to low or simmer.

NOTE: Cooking times are all approximate.

VEGETABLES	PREPARATION and SERVING
Asparagus Amount: 1 lb. Makes: 2 servings	Cut and discard tough ends. Cook 15 - 20 minutes whole or10 minutes if cut in pieces. Drizzle with melted butter or cheese sauce.
Beans (Green or Yellow) Amount: 1/2 lb. Makes: 2 servings	Snip off ends and remove string if any. Cook 20 - 30 minutes whole or 20 minutes if cut in pieces. Put 1 tsp. butter over beans and let melt.
Beets Amount: 1 lb. Makes: 2 servings	Cut off top leaves. Peel and wash beets. Slice into1/2" size pieces and boil for15 - 20 minutes. Drain. Add salt, butter and 1 tbsp. honey if desired.
Broccoli Amount: 1 lb. Makes: 2 servings	Cut off large leaves and tough ends. Slit stem lengthwise 1/2" thick. Cook 10 -15 minutes. Pour melted butter or cheese sauce over broccoli.
Brussels Sprouts Amount: 1/2 lb. Makes: 2 servings	Remove wilted leaves. Cut off stem ends. Wash. Cook whole for 10 - 20 minutes. Drizzle melted butter or lemon juice over sprouts. Also try chopped parsley or chives.

Carrots Amount: 1/2 lb. Makes: 2 servings	Scrub, scrape or thinly peel. Cook whole 20 - 30 min. Slices or pieces cook for 15 minutes. Add butter, chopped parsley or chives. Add salt and pepper to taste.
Cauliflower Amount: 1 small Makes: 2 servings	Remove outer leaves. Cut off blemishes and wash. Cook whole for 20 - 30 minutes or in pieces for 8 - 10 minutes. Serve with butter, grated cheese or cheese sauce.
Celery Amount: 1 1/3 cups Makes: 2 servings	Cut off leaves, trim roots. Wash thoroughly and cut diagonally. Cook for 10 - 15 minutes. Saute in butter or smother in a cream sauce.
Corn on the cob Amount: 4 cobs Makes: 2 servings	Remove husks and silk. Boil for 5 - 8 minutes. Serve with salt and butter.
Peas Amount: 1 lb. Makes: 2 servings	Shell and wash before cooking. Cook 10 - 15 minutes. Melt 1 tbsp. of butter over top.
Potatoes Amount: 1 lb. Makes: 2 servings	Scrub well. Remove blemishes. Cook with skins on for 35 minutes or peeled for 20 - 25 minutes. May be pan fried, mashed or baked. Serve with butter, sour cream, chives and bacon bits.
Spinach and Greens Amount: 1 lb. Makes: 2 servings	Discard stem ends, tough stalks and yellow leaves. Wash in warm water. Cook for approximately 10 minutes. Cut cooked greens before serving. Sprinkle with lemon juice or vinegar and butter.

Turnips	Scrub well. Peel and cut into cubes or
Amount: 1 lb.	strips. Cook about 15 - 20 minutes.
Makes: 2 servings	

Tomatoes	Wash, scald and slip the skin off. Quarter
Amount: 2 lbs.	and cook without water for 5 - 10 minutes.
Makes: 2 servings	

FRIED POTATOES

TEMP: medium
COOKING TIME: 15 minutes
PREPARATION TIME: 10 minutes
MAKES: 1 serving

INGREDIENTS:
2 medium potatoes
2 tbsp. onion, chopped
1/4 tsp. salt
2 tbsp. cooking oil
2 tbsp. butter

DIRECTIONS:
1. Peel and slice potatoes in thin slices.
2. Heat oil in a frying pan to medium hot.
3. Add butter to frying pan.
4. Add potatoes, onions and salt to taste.
5. Stir occasionally so as not to burn potatoes.
6. Cook until golden brown and soft.

Serve with hamburgers.

NOTE: For extra servings increase all ingredients.

CRISPY OVEN POTATOES

TEMP: 400 degrees
COOKING TIME: 45 minutes
PREPARATION TIME: 10 minutes
MAKES: 4 servings

INGREDIENTS:
6 medium potatoes
2 tbsp. vegetable oil
3 tbsp. melted butter
3/4 tsp. salt
1/4 tsp. thyme
1/8 tsp. pepper

OPTIONAL: 2 tbsp. parsley.

DIRECTIONS:
1. Wash and peel potatoes.
2. Slice potatoes thinly and sprinkle with salt.
3. Arrange potatoes in greased 8" x 8" baking pan.
4. Combine remaining ingredients and pour over potatoes.
5. Cover with foil and bake 30 minutes.
6. Remove foil and bake another 15 minutes or until tender.
7. Serve immediately.

BASIC BOILED OR MASHED POTATO

TEMP: medium - high
COOKING TIME: 20 - 30 minutes
PREPARATION TIME: 5 minutes
MAKES: 4 servings

INGREDIENTS:
4 large potatoes, peeled and quartered   2 tbsp. butter
1 cup water   1/2 cup cream or milk
1/2 tsp. salt

DIRECTIONS:
1. Peel and quarter potatoes. Place in medium-sized pot.
2. Add water and salt, cover with lid.
3. When water boils turn heat to low and cook until tender.
   (approximately 20 - 30 minutes).
4. Drain and serve.
5. Mash with approximately 2 tbsp. butter and 1/2 cup cream or milk.
   Beat until all lumps are gone and potatoes are creamy smooth.

POTATO SKINS

TEMP: 400 degrees
COOKING TIME: 1 hour
PREPARATION TIME: 15 minutes
MAKES: 1 potato makes 4 pieces

INGREDIENTS:

potatoes
bacon bits
cheddar cheese, grated
melted butter

cooking oil
green onions, chopped
sour cream

DIRECTIONS:
1. Scrub and pierce potatoes, then rub with cooking oil.
2. Bake for 1 hour at 400 degrees.
3. Cut potatoes into quarters.
4. Scoop most of potato out leaving about 1/8" on skin.
5. Brush potatoes inside and out with butter.
6. Place on cookie sheet and bake at 400 degrees until crisp.
7. Remove and sprinkle generously with bacon bits, onions and
   cheese, then bake until cheese melts.

NOTE: Serve with sour cream. Use scooped out potatoes in easy
potato cake or carrot potato fritters next day.

PRINCESS POTATOES

TEMP: 375 degrees
COOKING TIME: 1 hour
PREPARATION TIME: 10 minutes
MAKES: 6 - 8 servings

INGREDIENTS:

6 cups raw potatoes, grated
1/2 cup melted butter
1 1/4 cups onion, chopped
1/4 cup parsley, chopped

1 cup celery, chopped
1 tsp. salt
1/2 tsp. paprika

DIRECTIONS:
1. Peel and grate potatoes.
2. Mix all ingredients together.
3. Put into well buttered 2-quart casserole dish.
4. Bake 1 hour.

STOVE-TOP SCALLOPED POTATOES

TEMP: low - medium
COOKING TIME: 15 - 20 minutes
PREPARATION TIME: 15 minutes
MAKES: 4 servings

INGREDIENTS:

6 medium potatoes
1 1/2 cups milk or water
1 clove garlic, crushed
1/2 - 1 cup onions, chopped

3 tbsp. butter
1/2 tsp. salt
1/4 tsp. pepper
1 1/2 cups cheese, grated

OPTIONAL: Use cheese you like best.

DIRECTIONS:
1. Peel and slice potatoes thinly or in small cubes.
2. Combine potatoes with rest of ingredients except cheese.
3. Bring to a boil.
4. Cover, reduce heat to a simmer and cook until tender. Stir often to prevent sticking. Add a little extra water or milk if it gets too thick.
5. Grease an 8" square baking pan.
6. Place cooked potatoes in pan.
7. Stir 1/2 cup of the cheese into potatoes.
8. Sprinkle remaining cheese on top.
9. Place dish 6" from preheated broiler and broil until golden, about 10 minutes.

OVEN FRIED POTATOES

TEMP: 350 degrees
COOKING TIME: 30 minutes
PREPARATION TIME: 10 minutes
MAKES: 4 servings

INGREDIENTS:
4 potatoes
2 tbsp. oil
salt (to taste)

OPTIONAL: Garlic powder or onion salt.

DIRECTIONS:
1. Slice potatoes 1/8" thick and place on oiled cookie sheet.
2. Sprinkle with salt and bake until done, about 30 minutes.

MEAL IN A SPUD

TEMP: 400 degrees
COOKING TIME: 20 miinutes
PREPARATION TIME: 15 minutes
MAKES: 4 servings

INGREDIENTS:

4 large baked potatoes	1/4 cup cottage cheese
7 oz. can salmon	1 green onion, chopped
3/4 cup cheddar cheese, grated	1/4 cup mayonnaise

OPTIONAL: 2 tbsp. chopped parsley, additional cheddar cheese for topping.

DIRECTIONS:
1. Slice the top off the baked potatoes.
2. Scoop out pulp (potato).
3. Combine pulp with salmon (deboned) including juices.
4. Add remaining ingredients except cheddar cheese reserved for topping.
5. Mix lightly but thoroughly.
6. Spoon mixture back into potato shells.
7. Bake at 400 degrees for 10 minutes.
8. Top with reserved cheese and bake another 10 minutes or until cheese melts.
9. Serve HOT.

BAKED POTATO

TEMP: 375 degrees
COOKING TIME: 1 hour
PREPARATION TIME: 10 minutes

INGREDIENTS:
1 potato per person

OPTIONAL: May also be served with sour cream, bacon bits or chives.

DIRECTIONS:
1. Wash and scrub potatoes. Pierce skin of each potato with a fork 3 - 4 times.
2. Wrap potato in tin foil and bake until tender.
3. Serve with butter.

NOTE: Do not wrap in foil if you want a potato with a crisp skin.

CREAMY SCALLOPED POTATOES

TEMP: 375 degrees
COOKING TIME: 1 hour 15 minutes
PREPARATION TIME: 15 minutes
MAKES: 4 servings

INGREDIENTS:
5 cups sliced raw potatoes
10 oz. can cream of mushroom soup, undiluted
1/2 cup milk
1 medium onion, chopped

DIRECTIONS:
1. Mix the soup with the milk and onion.
2. Butter a casserole dish.
3. Alternate potatoes and soup in layers in the casserole dish.
4. Cover and bake 1 hour, uncover and bake an additional 15 minutes.

NOTE: Serve with green salad and meat dish.

POTATOES AND CHEESE

TEMP: 350 degrees
COOKING TIME: 30 minutes
PREPARATION TIME: 15 minutes
MAKES: 4 servings

INGREDIENTS:
4 potatoes
2 tbsp. butter or margarine
3 - 4 tbsp. Cheese Whiz or grated cheese

OPTIONAL: Sliced onions.

DIRECTIONS:
1. Wash and peel potatoes and cut into 1/2 inch cubes.
2. Arrange potato cubes and onion slices on aluminum foil.
3. Dab with butter and Cheese Whiz. Close foil.
4. Preheat oven and bake for about 30 minutes.

NOTE: May be cooked on the barbecue. Serve with barbecued
steak or chicken, and a salad.

EASY POTATO CAKE ═══════

TEMP: 425 degrees
COOKING TIME: 30 - 40 minutes
PREPARATION TIME: 10 minutes
MAKES: 4 servings

INGREDIENTS:

2 cups mashed potatoes (leftovers)
5 - 6 eggs, beaten
1/2 tsp. garlic or onion salt

1 tsp. baking powder
1/2 cup milk or cream
1 tsp. salt

OPTIONAL: 1/2 cup chopped onions, 1 tbsp. parsley or dill.

DIRECTIONS:
1. Beat eggs and add all the remaining ingredients and be sure that all powders and salts are mixed well.
2. Add above mixture to mashed potatoes and mix well again.
3. Pour into buttered 2-quart baking pan. Bake for 30 - 40 minutes.
4. Serve with melted butter or sour cream.

POTATO CUTLETS ═══════

TEMP: medium - high
COOKING TIME: 20 - 30 minutes
PREPARATION TIME: 20 minutes
MAKES: 5 servings

INGREDIENTS:

5 potatoes, grated
2 onions, finely chopped
2 eggs, beaten
1 cup crushed crackers

2 tbsp. oil
1/2 tsp. salt
1/4 tsp. pepper

DIRECTIONS:
1. Mix together first four ingredients.
2. Add salt and pepper.
3. Mix well and form into patties.
4. Fry in oil on both sides for about 20 - 30 minutes or until cooked thoroughly.

NOTE: Serve with tomato and cucumber salad or steamed vegetables.

CARROT POTATO FRITTERS ▬▬▬

TEMP: medium - high
COOKING TIME: 10 minutes
MAKES: 2 servings

INGREDIENTS:

1 cup cooked carrots, mashed
1/2 cup cooked potatoes, mashed
1/2 cup onion, chopped

1 clove garlic, crushed
1 tbsp. ketchup
1 tsp. oil

OPTIONAL: 1/2 tsp. dill.

DIRECTIONS:
1. Saute onion and garlic in oil.
2. Mix all ingredients in a bowl and shape into patties.
3. Cook in non-stick pan until browned.
4. Turn and brown on other side.

ORANGE-GLAZED CARROTS ▬▬▬

TEMP: medium
COOKING TIME: approximately 15 minutes
PREPARATION TIME: 10 minutes
MAKES: 3 servings

INGREDIENTS:
3 - 4 medium carrots, peeled
1/4 cup butter
2 tbsp. sugar or honey
1/8 tsp. salt
juice and grated rind of 1 small orange

DIRECTIONS:
1. Cut carrots into 1" slices.
2. Cook in 1" of salted water until tender. Drain.
3. Combine butter, sugar, salt and orange juice in saucepan.
4. Cook until syrup is thickened.
5. Add grated rind.
6. Pour over carrots.

NOTE: Serve with a meat dish and a salad.

GARDEN CHOW MEIN

TEMP: medium - high
COOKING TIME: 15 minutes
PREPARATION TIME: 20 minutes
MAKES: 4 servings

INGREDIENTS:
3 tbsp. oil
1 medium onion, sliced
2 cups mushrooms, sliced
2 stalks celery, washed and sliced
200 gr. pkg. chow mein noodles
1 carrot, grated

1/2 lb. bean sprouts, washed
1/2 tsp. salt
1/4 tsp. garlic powder
1 green pepper, sliced
1/4 cup water

OPTIONAL: 1 small bok choy, washed and sliced in 1" pieces.

SAUCE INGREDIENTS:
1 1/2 tbsp. cornstarch
2 tbsp. soya sauce
3/4 cup water

DIRECTIONS:
1. In hot wok or large frying pan, heat oil and fry onion until translucent.
2. Add remaining ingredients, except for chow mein noodles, and mix.
3. Cover and cook about 5 minutes until vegetables are crisp and tender.
4. Add chow mein noodles. Stir and steam for 3 minutes more.
5. Mix sauce ingredients and add to vegetables and noodles. Stir until thickened and blended.
6. Serve immediately with sesame seeds and more soya sauce.

SOUPER RICE

TEMP: medium
COOKING TIME: approximately 20 minutes
PREPARATION TIME: 5 minutes
MAKES: 4 servings

INGREDIENTS:
2 cups cold water
1 cup uncooked rice
1 package onion or onion/mushroom soup mix
1 tbsp. butter or margarine

OPTIONAL: Any favourite soup may be used.

DIRECTIONS:

1. Stir soup mix and water in saucepan.
2. Bring to a boil, stirring occasionally.
3. Add butter or margarine and the rice.
4. Bring to a full boil, occasionally lifting rice with a fork (rather than stirring).
5. Cover with tight-fitting lid and cook over low - medium heat for approximately 20 minutes. Do not uncover while cooking.
6. Fluff with fork and serve.

FRIED RICE

TEMP: medium - high
COOKING TIME: 30 minutes
PREPARATION TIME: 15 minutes
MAKES: 4 servings

INGREDIENTS:
1/4 cup onion, chopped
2 tbsp. green pepper, chopped
10 oz. can sliced mushrooms
1 cup uncooked rice

2 tbsp. salad oil
2 tbsp. soya sauce
3 eggs, beaten

OPTIONAL: 1/2 cup cubed ham.

DIRECTIONS:
1. Cook rice according to package directions.
2. In large frying pan, cook and stir onion and pepper in oil until tender.
3. Stir in rice, mushrooms and soya sauce. Add eggs.
4. Cook over low heat, stirring frequently, until egg is cooked.

RICE

TEMP: medium - high
COOKING TIME: approximatley 20 minutes
PREPARATION TIME: 5 minutes
MAKES: 4 servings

INGREDIENTS:

1 cup uncooked rice	1 tsp. salt
2 cups cold water	1 tsp. butter

DIRECTIONS:
1. Combine rice, water, salt and butter in a 3-quart saucepan that has a tight-fitting lid.
2. Bring to a boil uncovered, lifting rice (rather than stirring) once or twice as water comes to boil. Lower heat to simmer.
3. Cover pan and cook about 20 minutes without removing lid or stirring.

VEGETABLE MEDLEY

TEMP: medium
COOKING TIME: 10 minutes
PREPARATION TIME: 10 minutes
MAKES: 4 servings

INGREDIENTS:

1 large carrot	1/4 lb. mushrooms
1 celery stalk	3/4 tsp. salt
1 onion	1/8 cup salad oil
1 small bunch broccoli	

DIRECTIONS:
1. Cut carrot in half or thirds and then in matchstick strips.
2. Cut celery stalk in matchstick pieces of about 2" long.
3. Slice onion and mushrooms.
4. Cut broccoli into 2" pieces.
5. Heat salad oil in frying pan.
6. Add all vegetables, fry 2 - 3 minutes, stirring frequently.
7. Add 1/8 cup water, 3/4 tsp. salt and cook covered about 5 minutes or until tender crisp.

GLAZED VEGETABLES

TEMP: medium - high
COOKING TIME: 30 minutes
PREPARATION TIME: 15 minutes
MAKES: 6 servings

INGREDIENTS:

1/4 cup honey
2 tbsp. butter
2 tbsp. lemon juice
1 tsp. Worcestershire sauce

1 tsp. vinegar
1/4 tsp. salt
3 cups beets or carrots,
    sliced and cooked

DIRECTIONS:

1. In a large frying pan, combine all ingredients except vegetables.
2. Bring to a boil, stirring occasionally.
3. Boil 1 minute, reduce heat and add vegetables.
4. Simmer just until vegetables are heated through, stirring occasionaly.
5. With a slotted spoon, remove vegetables to serving dish and pour glaze over top.

BASIC ZUCCHINI PARMIGIANA

TEMP: 350 degrees
COOKING TIME: 15 minutes
PREPARATION TIME: 30 minutes
MAKES: 4 servings

INGREDIENTS:

2 1/2 cups canned tomatoes
3 tbsp. tomato paste
1/4 cup oil
2 medium zucchini, sliced
2 cups bread crumbs
1 tbsp. basil

1 tbsp. salt
1/2 tsp. pepper
2 tbsp. parsley
1/3 cup parmesan cheese
1 clove garlic, crushed
8 oz. mozzarella, sliced

DIRECTIONS:

1. Simmer tomatoes and tomato paste for 25 minutes.
2. Saute zucchini in oil until soft.
3. Combine bread crumbs, parsley, parmesan, garlic and spices.
4. Grease 1 1/2-quart baking dish.
5. Layer half the zucchini, then follow with the bread mixture, tomato sauce and mozzarella. Repeat.
6. Bake for 15 minutes in preheated oven.

EGGS MEXICAN STYLE

TEMP: medium
COOKING TIME: 15 minutes
PREPARATION TIME: 5 minutes
MAKES: 2 - 4 servings

INGREDIENTS:
4 eggs
2 dozen tortilla chips
1 tbsp. butter

HOT SAUCE INGREDIENTS:
2 cups canned tomatoes
1 small green pepper, chopped
2 tsp. onion, chopped
1 tbsp. lemon juice

1 clove garlic, minced
1 tsp. oregano
1/8 tsp. cayenne pepper

OPTIONAL: 1/4 tsp. allspice, 1/8 tsp. Tabasco sauce.

DIRECTIONS:
1. Combine all sauce ingredients in a saucepan.
2. Bring to a boil and simmer 15 minutes.
3. While sauce cooks, line serving plates with tortilla chips.
4. Put butter in skillet on medium heat.
5. Break in eggs. Add 2 tsp. water to skillet and cover.
6. Lower heat and cook eggs 2 - 3 minutes.
7. Lift onto tortilla chips, surround with hot sauce and serve.

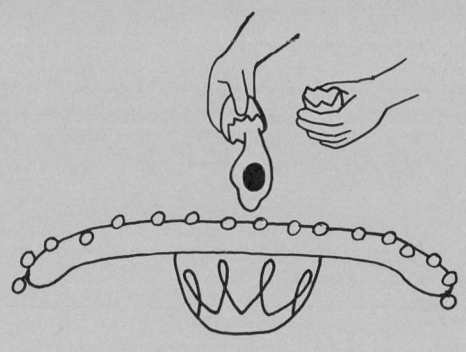

TOFU CHILI

TEMP: medium
COOKING TIME: 35 minutes
PREPARATION TIME: 10 minutes
MAKES: 4 - 6 servings

INGREDIENTS:

2 tbsp. oil
1 large onion, chopped
1 green pepper, chopped
1 clove of garlic, minced
1 tsp. chili powder
1/2 tsp. oregano
1 cup cheddar cheese, grated

1/4 tsp. black pepper
3 cups canned tomatoes
7 oz. can sliced mushrooms
38 oz. can kidney beans
1/2 lb. tofu, cut in cubes
5 oz. can tomato paste
1/2 tsp. salt

DIRECTIONS:

1. Heat oil in a 5-quart cooking pot over medium heat.
2. Saute onion, green pepper and garlic until onion is translucent.
3. Add mushrooms (drained), chili powder, oregano, salt and pepper. Cook approximately 2 minutes.
4. Stir in tomatoes and tomato paste. Bring to a boil.
5. Reduce heat and simmer uncovered 15 minutes.
6. Stir in kidney beans and tofu. Simmer another 15 minutes.
7. Add 1/2 cup shredded cheese. Stir until cheese melts.
8. Serve in bowls and sprinkle with remaining 1/2 cup of cheese.

VEGETARIAN CHILI

TEMP: low
COOKING TIME: 30 minutes
PREPARATION TIME: 20 minutes
MAKES: 4 - 6 servings

INGREDIENTS:

14 oz can kidney beans
14 oz. can baked beans
1/2 cup onions, chopped
1/2 cup green pepper, chopped
1/2 cup celery, chopped

2 cloves of garlic, minced
10 oz. can mushrooms
8 oz. can tomatoes
1 tsp. chili powder
1/2 cup chili sauce

DIRECTIONS:

1. Simmer all ingredients together for 30 minutes or until vegetables are cooked.

VEGETARIAN LASAGNE

TEMP: 375 degrees
COOKING TIME: 35 - 40 minutes
PREPARATION TIME: 30 minutes
MAKES: 6 - 8 servings

INGREDIENTS:
8 lasagne noodles
8 oz. mozzarella cheese, grated
2 cups creamed cottage cheese
2 eggs
1/8 tsp. salt
1/4 tsp. black pepper

OPTIONAL: 2 tsp. parsley.

SAUCE INGREDIENTS:
1 onion, chopped
2 cloves garlic, finely chopped
1/2 lb. mushrooms, chopped
2 medium zucchini
28 oz. can meatless spaghetti sauce

1/2 tsp. basil
1/2 tsp. oregano
1 tsp. sugar
1/4 cup butter
14 oz. can tomato sauce

DIRECTIONS:
1. Cut unpeeled zucchini into thin strips.
2. Melt butter in frying pan. Stir-fry zucchini for approximately 5 minutes.
3. Put fried zucchini into a bowl. Add mushrooms, onion and garlic to frying pan and stir fry approximately 3 minutes.
4. Return zucchini to pan and add all other sauce ingredients.
5. Cover, reduce heat and simmer 20 minutes.
6. While sauce simmers, cook lasagne noodles according to pack age directions. When cooked, run cold water over noodles. Drain.
7. Beat eggs lightly, mixing in cottage cheese, salt, pepper and parsley.
8. Butter a 9" x 12" baking dish or pan.
9. Cover bottom with a little sauce. Add a layer of noodles, a layer of cottage cheese mixture, sauce and finally grated mozzarella. Repeat layering until you end up with sauce and mozzarella on top.
10. Bake at 375° for 35 - 40 minutes.

VEGETARIAN BURGER

TEMP: broil
COOKING TIME: 10 minutes
PREPARATION TIME: 10 minutes
MAKES: 2 servings

INGREDIENTS:

1/2 cup rice, cooked
3 mushrooms, chopped
1/4 cup onions, chopped
1/8 cup dry bread crumbs
1 egg

pepper to taste
1 garlic clove, crushed
3/4 tsp. soya sauce
1/4 tsp. salt

DIRECTIONS:
1. Mix everything together and shape into patties.

NO CRUST CARROT QUICHE

TEMP: 350 degrees
COOKING TIME: 35 - 40 minutes
PREPARATION TIME: 15 minutes
MAKES: 4 servings

INGREDIENTS:

2 cups cooked carrots, sliced
6 eggs
2 cups creamed cottage cheese
1 small onion, chopped
1 cup cheddar cheese, grated

1/2 tsp. dried dillweed
1/4 tsp. salt
1/8 tsp. pepper
1 clove of garlic, minced

OPTIONAL: 1 1/2 tsp. fresh dill instead of dried dillweed, Swiss or mozzarella instead of cheddar cheese.

DIRECTIONS:
1. Cook sliced carrots until tender. Drain and mash.
2. In a large bowl, blend eggs, cottage cheese, onion, garlic, dill, salt and pepper until smooth.
3. Add carrots and cheese.
4. Pour into greased 10" quiche pan or pie plate.
5. Bake 35 - 40 minutes until mixture is set and lightly browned.
6. Let stand 10 minutes and cut in wedges.

BROCCOLI - CHEESE BAKE ═══════════

TEMP: 350 degrees
COOKING TIME: 35 minutes
PREPARATION TIME: 15 minutes
MAKES: 4 servings

INGREDIENTS:

20 oz. frozen broccoli
4 eggs
1 cup milk
1 cup flour

1 tsp. baking powder
1 tsp. salt
2 tbsp. onion, chopped
2 cups cheese, grated

DIRECTIONS:
1. Steam broccoli about 3 minutes.
2. Drain, cool and pat dry with paper towel.
3. Beat eggs and milk.
4. Add flour, baking powder and salt to eggs and milk. Mix.
5. Fold in broccoli, onion and cheese.
6. Pour into buttered casserole dish and bake.

CAULIFLOWER ALMONDINE ═══════════

TEMP: 325 degrees
COOKING TIME: 10 minutes
PREPARATION TIME: 15 minutes
MAKES: 4 servings

INGREDIENTS:

16 oz. cauliflower
1/4 tsp. salt
10 oz. can cream of mushroom soup

1/4 cup slivered almonds
1 tbsp. melted butter
2 tbsp. bread crumbs

DIRECTIONS:
1. Cook cauliflower in 1/4 cup of salted water until tender (4 - 5 minutes).
2. Drain and arrange in a small casserole dish.
3. Heat undiluted soup and stir in almonds.
4. Pour over cauliflower.
5. Mix butter and crumbs and spread over cauliflower.
6. Preheat oven and bake 10 minutes.

ZUCCHINI QUICHE

TEMP: 450 degrees
COOKING TIME: 40 minutes
PREPARATION TIME: 15 minutes
MAKES: 4 servings

INGREDIENTS:
2 cups zucchini, chopped
1/4 cup onion, chopped
2 tbsp. oil
1 1/2 cups mozzarella cheese, grated
2 eggs

1 1/4 cups milk
1 tbsp. flour
1/4 tsp. salt
1/8 tsp. pepper
pie shell, unbaked
(see recipe below)

OPTIONAL: 1 sliced tomato, celery or green pepper.

DIRECTIONS:
1. Saute zucchini, onion, celery and green pepper until tender.
   Set aside.
2. Sprinkle cheese in bottom of unbaked pie shell.
3. Pour zucchini/vegetable mixture on top.
4. Mix remaining ingredients.
5. Pour over zucchini/vegetable mixture.
6. Bake at 450 degrees for 10 minutes.
7. Reduce heat to 350 degrees and bake for 30 minutes.

PIE SHELL

PREPARATION TIME: 15 minutes
MAKES: 1 pie shell

INGREDIENTS:
1 cup flour
1/2 tsp. salt
1/2 cup shortening
2 tbsp. ice water

DIRECTIONS:
1. Mix flour and salt in mixing bowl.
2. Cut shortening into flour with 2 knives or pastry blender.
3. Sprinkle ice water over flour and mix with fork.
4. Turn out onto floured surface and form into a ball.
   (Handle as little as possible).
5. Roll out with rolling pin to 1/8" thickness and put into a 9-inch pie
   plate.
6. Trim edges.

CASSEROLES ═

EASY & ELEGANT CHEESE SOUFFLÉ ═══

TEMP: 350 degrees
COOKING TIME: 1 hour
PREPARATION TIME: 40 minutes
MAKES: 2 servings

INGREDIENTS:

4 slices bread, halved
3 cups cheddar cheese, grated
2 cups milk
3 eggs, beaten
1/2 tsp. Worcestershire sauce

1/2 tsp. salt
1/2 tsp. thyme
1/2 tsp. dry mustard
few grains black pepper
butter

DIRECTIONS:
1. Layer the cheese and bread in a buttered 6-cup baking dish, starting with the bread.
2. Beat the eggs, milk, salt and remaining ingredients and pour over the bread layer. Let stand 30 minutes.
3. Place baking dish into a cake pan which has been filled with 1/2" of hot water. Bake at 350 degrees for 1 hour.

MACARONI CASSEROLE ═══════

TEMP: 350 degrees
COOKING TIME: 20 minutes
PREPARATION TIME: 20 minutes
MAKES: 4 servings

INGREDIENTS:

1 1/2 cups macaroni
2 quarts water
1 1/2 oz. pkg. spaghetti sauce mix
1/2 lb. ground beef
1 small onion, chopped

7 1/2 oz. can tomato sauce
2 1/2 cups canned tomatoes
1 tbsp. salt
2 tbsp. butter
2 cups cheese, grated

DIRECTIONS:
1. Boil water, add salt. Boil macaroni until tender. Drain.
2. Brown meat with onion.
3. Add spaghetti mix and tomatoes.
4. Simmer 20 minutes, stirring occasionally.
5. Mix with cooked macaroni.
6. Butter 9"x 9" pan, add macaroni mixture, spread cheese on top, and bake for 20 minutes.

CORNED BEEF 'N NOODLE BAKE ═══

TEMP: 350 degrees
COOKING TIME: 30 minutes
PREPARATION TIME: 20 minutes
MAKES: 4 - 6 servings

INGREDIENTS:

4 oz. wide noodles
3 tbsp. butter
3 tbsp. flour
2 cups milk
1 garlic clove, chopped

1 tsp. prepared mustard
12 oz. can corned beef
1 1/2 tsp. salt
1/4 tsp. black pepper

OPTIONAL: 1 tsp. horseradish and 1 cup peas.

DIRECTIONS:
1. Cook noodles according to package instructions. Drain.
2. In saucepan, melt butter and add flour.
3. Add milk slowly, and cook, stirring constantly until mixture thickens and bubbles.
4. Stir in garlic, mustard, salt, pepper and horseradish.
5. Add noodles and thawed peas.
6. Place into 8" x 8" x 2 " baking dish.
7. Cut corned beef into 6 slices and arrange on top of noodle mixture.
8. Bake at 350 degrees for 30 minutes.

FRENCH BEAN CASSEROLE ═══

TEMP: 350 degrees
COOKING TIME: 20 minutes
PREP. TIME: 10 minutes
MAKES: 4 - 6 servings

INGREDIENTS:

14 oz. French cut green beans, drained
1/4 cup almonds, slivered
1/2 can cream of mushroom soup
1/2 cup bread or cracker crumbs

DIRECTIONS:
1. Place beans in one-quart baking dish. Fold in almonds and soup.
2. Sprinkle with crumbs. Bake at 350 degrees about 20 minutes.

NOTE: Dilute leftover half can of soup with half a can of water and serve as soup.

EASY EGG POT PIE

TEMP: 400 degrees
COOKING TIME: 25 minutes
PREPARATION TIME: 15 minutes
MAKES: 4 - 6 servings

INGREDIENTS:
11 oz. package frozen mixed vegetables
1 cup diced celery
8 hard boiled eggs, chopped
10 oz. can cream of mushroom soup
1/4 tsp. pepper
1/4 tsp. garlic powder
1/4 tsp. salt
8 oz. biscuit dough

OPTIONAL: 1/4 tsp. dried dill.

DIRECTIONS:
1. Cook frozen vegetables according to package directions until tender crisp.
2. Drain and spread in shallow 2-quart casserole dish.
3. Top with diced celery and chopped eggs.
4. Blend soup and seasonings and pour over mixture.
5. Lift vegetable/egg mixture with spoon to allow soup mixture to penetrate. Bake at 400 degrees for 10 minutes.
6. Mix biscuit dough according to package directions.
7. Take casserole out and place biscuits on top of casserole and bake an additional 10 - 15 minutes or until biscuits are browned and casserole is hot and bubbly.

MACARONI & CHEESE FOR A CROWD

TEMP: 350 degrees
COOKING TIME: 45 minutes
PREPARATION TIME: 20 minutes
MAKES: enough for 12 - 16 people

INGREDIENTS:
6 cups uncooked macaroni
3/4 cup butter
1/2 cup flour
2 tsp. salt
1/4 tsp. black pepper

8 cups milk
1 cup onion, chopped
2 tbsp. butter
1 1/2 lbs. cheese, cubed
4 tomatoes, sliced

DIRECTIONS:
1. Preheat oven to 350 degrees.
2. Cook macaroni according to package directions, in a large pot of salted water. Drain.
3. Melt butter in large pot. Blend in flour, salt and pepper.
4. Add milk and cook, stirring constantly until thick and bubbly.
5. Saute onion in butter in frying pan.
6. Add onion and cheese to milk mixture. Stir until cheese melts.
7. Spread macaroni in two 13" x 9" x 2" glass or metal pans.
8. Add half the sauce to each pan. Mix with macaroni.
9. Arrange tomato slices on top, then salt lightly and bake about 45 minutes or until bubbly in the centre.

TUNA FISH CASSEROLE

TEMP: 350 degrees
COOKING TIME: 30 minutes
PREPARATION TIME: 5 minutes
MAKES: enough for 8 slices of toast

INGREDIENTS:
7 oz. can solid or flaked white tuna
10 oz. can cream of mushroom soup

14 oz. can peas
8 slices bread, toasted

DIRECTIONS:
1. Drain liquid from peas and tuna.
2. Cut solid tuna into small chunks.
3. Mix tuna, soup, and peas together in casserole dish.
4. Cover and bake until mixture is hot (about 20 - 30 minutes).
5. Spread on slices of toasted bread and serve immediately.

DEEP DISH CHICKEN PIE ═══════════

TEMP: 350 degrees
COOKING TIME: 30 minutes
PREPARATION TIME: 30 minutes
MAKES: 4 servings

INGREDIENTS:

1 cup carrots	1/4 cup green pepper
1 cup potatoes	1 tbsp. butter
10 oz. can cream of mushroom soup	1/4 cup onions
1 1/2 cups leftover cooked chicken	biscuit topping (see below)

OPTIONAL: 1/4 cup cooked green peas, cream of chicken soup.

DIRECTIONS:
1. Peel and cube the carrots and potatoes.
2. Cook in salted water for 15 minutes and drain, saving 3/4 cup of liquid.
3. Saute chopped onion and green pepper in butter.
4. Stir in cream soup and saved liquid.
5. Spoon vegetables and chicken into 2-quart casserole dish.
6. Pour soup mixture over top. Preheat oven and bake at 350 degrees for 15 minutes (while making biscuit topping).
7. Arrange biscuit topping on hot mixture.
8. Bake another 15 minutes or until golden brown.

BISCUIT TOPPING ═══════════

INGREDIENTS:
1 1/2 cups flour
2 tsp. baking powder
1/2 tsp. salt
1/4 cup butter or margarine
1/2 cup milk

DIRECTIONS:
1. Mix flour, salt and baking powder in medium-sized bowl.
2. Cut in butter.
3. Add milk, stir just until blended.
4. Turn out dough on lightly floured board, knead 1/2 minute.
5. Roll out to 7" round, cut into wedges or squares.
6. Arrange biscuit on hot mixture.
7. Brush lightly with milk and bake until golden brown.

MOM'S BEST PASTA PRIMAVERA ▬▬▬

TEMP: medium - high
COOKING TIME: 15 minutes
PREPARATION TIME: 20 minutes
MAKES: 4 servings

INGREDIENTS:

1/2 lb. linguine	2 tbsp. parsley
1/2 lb. broccoli pieces	1/8 tsp. pepper
1 cup cauliflower pieces	3/4 tsp. salt
1 cup carrot pieces	3/4 tsp. basil
1/2 cup frozen peas	1/8 cup butter
1 onion	1/2 cup whipping cream
2 cloves garlic	1/2 cup parmesan cheese
1/4 lb. fresh mushrooms	1/8 cup oil

OPTIONAL: Other pastas may be substituted; 1 small zucchini.

DIRECTIONS:
1. Cook linguine according to package directions.
2   Wash and slice into pieces the broccoli, cauliflower, carrots and zucchini.
3   Boil above vegetables with peas until tender. Drain.
4   In large frying pan, saute onion, garlic and mushrooms about 5 minutes.
5   Stir in parsley, salt, pepper and basil. Cook 1 more minute and add to vegetables.
6   In same pan melt butter. Add cream and cheese. Cook until smooth.
7   Add linguine. Toss.
8   Stir in vegetables and heat.

NOTE: Serve with garlic bread. When cooking pasta, add about 1 tbsp. vegetable oil to water to keep pasta from sticking together.

RICE & CHICKEN CASSEROLE
(use leftovers)

TEMP: 350 degrees or medium - high
COOKING TIME: 20 - 30 minutes
PREPARATION TIME: 10 minutes
MAKES: 2 servings

INGREDIENTS:
1 cup cooked rice
1 cup cooked chicken, chopped
10 oz. can cream of mushroom soup, undiluted

OPTIONAL: Use leftovers. Substitute cream of chicken soup for mushroom soup or fish or turkey for chicken. 1/4 cup chopped onion, 1 clove garlic, 2 sliced hard boiled eggs, 1/2 cup sliced mushrooms.

DIRECTIONS:
1. Mix everything together and heat in a frying pan or oven.

RICE CASSEROLE

TEMP: 350 degrees
COOKING TIME: 1 hour
PREPARATION TIME: 30 minutes
MAKES: 4 servings

INGREDIENTS:
1/2 cup long grain rice
1 lb. broccoli
10 oz. can cream of mushroom soup
10 oz. can sliced mushrooms, drained
1 1/2 cups cheddar cheese, grated

DIRECTIONS:
1. Cook rice according to package directions.
2. Cook broccoli until tender.
3. Spread half the rice in a 2-quart casserole, followed by a layer of broccoli.
4. Repeat with another layer of rice and broccoli.
5. Combine soup, 1 cup of cheese and mushrooms.
6. Spoon over top layer of broccoli. Bake for 50 minutes.
7. Sprinkle with remaining cheese and bake 10 minutes more.

PORK AND RICE CASSEROLE ====

TEMP: 350 degrees
COOKING TIME: 1 hour
PREPARATION TIME: 1/2 hour
MAKES: 4 servings

INGREDIENTS:
4 pork chops
1 tbsp. oil
1 cup rice, uncooked
1/4 cup onion, chopped
1/2 cup green pepper, chopped

10 oz. can consomme
1 cup water
1 tsp. salt
1/8 tsp. pepper

DIRECTIONS:
1. Heat oil in frying pan on medium heat. Brown chops in oil.
2. Place browned chops in 2-quart casserole dish.
3. Drain excess fat and lightly brown rice, onion and green pepper.
4. Spoon rice mixture over chops in casserole dish.
5. Add consomme, water, salt and pepper.

BEEF STROGANOFF ====

TEMP: low - medium
COOKING TIME: 1 hour 15 minutes
PREPARATION TIME: 15 minutes
MAKES: 4 servings

INGREDIENTS:
2 lbs. round steak
1/2 cup onions, chopped
1 clove garlic, minced
7 oz. can mushrooms, drained
1 tbsp. Worcestershire sauce
cooked noodles or spaghetti

6 drops Tabasco sauce
1/2 tsp. salt
1/4 tsp. pepper
1 cup sour cream
14 oz. can tomato soup
1/2 cup flour

DIRECTIONS:
1. Cut meat in cubes, coat with flour and brown in 2 tbsp. oil
2. Chop onions, mince garlic and drain mushrooms (save liquid). Add to meat.
3. Combine tomato soup, liquid from mushrooms and seasonings; pour over meat. Simmer until tender (approximately 1 hour).
4. Add sour cream, blend and heat (do not boil).
5. Serve over spaghetti or noodles and top with parmesan cheese if desired.

MACARONI DINNER
WITH CREAMED SALMON ====

TEMP: medium - high
COOKING TIME: 10 minutes
PREPARATION TIME: 20 minutes
MAKES: 4 servings

INGREDIENTS:
1 cup macaroni
1/2 tsp. salt
1/4 tsp. pepper
10 oz. can cream of celery or mushroom soup
1 cup milk
7 oz. can salmon
3 tbsp. butter or margarine
1 cup cheese, grated

DIRECTIONS:
1. Cook macaroni according to package directions.
2. Combine soup and milk in saucepan.
3. Heat soup and then blend in salmon (make sure salmon is drained and deboned).
4. Add seasonings and keep hot.
5. Drain cooked macaroni thoroughly. Do not rinse.
6. Add butter to drained macaroni.
7. Sprinkle cheese over macaroni. Mix again.
8. Serve immediately with hot, creamed salmon.

NOTE: Serve with salad or steamed vegetables.

CHEEZEE LASAGNA

TEMP: 350 degrees
COOKING TIME: 35 minutes
PREPARATION TIME: 30 minutes
MAKES: 6 servings

INGREDIENTS:

3/4 of 500 gr. package lasagna noodles
1 lb. ground beef
2 medium onions, chopped
1 cup celery, chopped
1 cup mushrooms, sliced
1/2 cup green pepper, chopped
3 cloves garlic, minced
1 tsp. oregano
2 cups grated mozzarella cheese

1 tbsp. butter or oil
2 cups canned tomatoes
5 1/2 oz. can tomato paste
1 tsp. salt
pepper to taste
2 cups cottage cheese
2 tbsp. parsley, chopped
2 eggs, well beaten

DIRECTIONS:
1. Cook noodles according to package directions, drain.
2. Saute onions, celery, mushrooms, green pepper and garlic in butter.
3. Add ground beef, oregano, salt, and pepper. Brown and stir.
4. Mix in tomatoes and tomato paste. Cook and stir 15 minutes over medium heat.
5. Grease 9" x 13" pan and line with layer of lasagna noodles.
6. Pour tomato/meat sauce over noodles.
7. Top with another layer of noodles.
8. Blend cottage cheese, eggs and parsley and spread over noodles.
9. Top with another layer of noodles.
10. Pour cheese sauce over lasagna. Recipe follows.
11. Sprinkle grated mozzarella cheese on top and bake for 35 minutes.

CHEESE SAUCE INGREDIENTS:
1/4 cup melted butter
1/2 cup flour
2 cups milk
1 cup cheddar cheese, grated
1/4 tsp. salt
pepper to taste

DIRECTIONS:
1. Melt butter, add flour, and stir well. Stir in milk slowly. Cook and stir over medium heat, until it starts to thicken. Add salt, pepper and cheddar cheese. Cook until it thickens. Pour over noodles.

MEAT
FISH and
POULTRY ———

THE LOW DOWN ON TURKEY ═══

THREE WAYS TO THAW:

1. In its original wrapping, on a tray in the refrigerator; 5 hours per lb.
   ie. A 12 lb. turkey would take 2 1/2 days to thaw.
2. Immerse in cold water; 1 hour per lb.
   ie. A 10 lb. turkey would take 10 hours.
3. In brown paper bag away from heat source; 1 1/2 hours per lb.
   ie. A 10 lb. turkey would take 15 hours.

TO ROAST:

1. Preheat oven to 325 degrees.
2. Place turkey on rack in roasting pan and rub skin with butter.
3. Cover with lid or foil, dull side out.
4. Roast, covered, basting often with pan juices.
5. The turkey is ready when drumstick moves easily.

STUFFED TURKEY:

WEIGHT	ROASTING TIME
4 lbs. or 1.75 kg	2 1/2 - 3 hours
8 lbs. or 3.5 kg	3 3/4 - 4 1/2 hours
16 lbs. or 7 kg	5 1/2 - 6 hours
20 lbs. or 9 kg	5 3/4 - 6 1/2 hours

NOTE: Unstuffed turkey takes about 1 hour less.

TO BROWN:
1. Remove cover for the last hour of roasting and baste often.
2. If the turkey browns unevenly, cover the dark spots with foil.

BEEF COOKING CHART ═══

STEAKS— TENDER CUTS	SIZE THICKNESS	COOKING TIME RARE / MEDIUM MINUTES
Sirloin Steak	1/2" - 3/4"	10 - 12 / 14 - 16
	1 1/4"	15 - 20 / 20 - 25
Porterhouse or T-Bone Steak	1/2" - 3/4"	9 - 10 / 12 - 15
	1" - 1 1/4"	15 - 18 / 20 - 30
Wing or Club Steak	1/2" - 3/4"	7 - 8 / 8 - 9
	1" - 1 1/4"	10 - 12 / 12 - 14
Tenderloin	1" - 1 1/4"	10 - 12 / 12 - 15

STEAKS—LESS TENDER CUTS	IN POUNDS	COOKING TIME
Swiss Steak	1 1/2 - 2 lb.	
Short Rib	2 1/2 - 3 lb.	2 - 2 1/2 hours
Round Steak	2 lb.	total time.

DIRECTIONS:

BROIL - Preheat broiler. Slash fat edge. Place on rack 4 - 5" below heat source. Broil half prescribed time on one side. Season. Turn with tongs. Broil other side.

PANBROIL - Slash fat edge. Grease pan and set over medium heat. Turn frequently to ensure even cooking.

BRAISE - Dip meat in seasoned flour. Brown on both sides in heavy pan with a little oil. Add 1/2 cup water, tomato juice, stock or any liquid. Cover tightly and cook in 300 degree oven or on top of stove until tender.

NOTE: For tender cuts broil or pan broil . Braise less tender cuts.

TIMETABLE FOR ROASTING BEEF

CUT	OVEN TEMPERATURE	APPROXIMATE COOKING TIME (minutes per lb.)
Standing Rib	300 - 325°	23 - 25 min. Rare
		27 - 30 min. Me-
dium		
		32 - 35 min. Well
Rolled Rib	300 - 325°	35 min. per lb. Rare
		40 min. per lb. Med.
		50 min. per lb. Well
Rump	300 - 325°	25 - 30 min. per lb.
Sirloin Tip	300 - 325°	25 - 30 min. per lb.

OPTIONAL INGREDIENTS:

1/2 tsp. garlic salt	1/4 cup cooking sherry
2 tbsp. onion soup mix	1/4 cup water

DIRECTIONS:

1. Wipe roast with clean damp cloth or a quick rinse under the tap.
2. Place in roaster or Dutch oven, fat side up.
3. Add optional ingredients (if desired).
4. Put into preheated oven, uncovered.

POT ROAST OF BEEF ═══════

TEMP: Low heat on stove top or 300 - 325 degree oven
COOKING TIME: 30 - 35 minutes per lb.
PREPARATION TIME: 15 minutes
MAKES: 4 - 6 servings

INGREDIENTS:
2 - 3 lb. roast (shoulder, chuck, blade, rump or brisket)
1/4 cup flour
1 tsp. salt
1/8 tsp. pepper
1 tbsp. oil
1 cup water or tomato juice

DIRECTIONS:
1. Rinse roast and wipe.
2. Dust meat with flour, salt, and pepper.
3. Heat oil in Dutch oven or pan (with tight lid).
4. Brown meat, add water or tomato juice and bring to a boil.
6. Turn down heat. Cover with tight fitting lid, and cook over low
    (simmer) heat until tender. Add more water if necessary.
7. If desired, make gravy with liquid left in pot by adding paste made
    with 2 tbsp. flour and 1/2 cup cold water.

BARBECUED STEAK ═══════

TEMP: red hot coals in barbecue
COOKING TIME: 10 min. rare, 20 min. medium, 30 min. well done
PREPARATION TIME: 15 minutes
MAKES: 1 serving

INGREDIENTS:
1/8 tsp. salt
1/8 tsp. pepper
1 steak

DIRECTIONS:
1. Wash meat under running water.
2. Place rack about 6" above coals.
3. Trim some fat off steaks and rub on rack to prevent steak
    from sticking.
4. Sprinkle both sides of steak with salt and pepper during cooking.
5. Cook until done as desired (ie.10 minutes rare = 5 minutes each
    side).

BARBECUED SPARERIBS

TEMP: 450 degrees
COOKING TIME: 2 hours
PREPARATION TIME: 15 minutes
MAKES: 4 servings

INGREDIENTS:
3 - 4 lbs. spareribs, cut in pieces
1 onion, thinly sliced
1 cup ketchup
1/3 cup Worcestershire sauce
1 tsp. chili powder
1 tsp. salt
1 1/2 cups water

OPTIONAL: 1 lemon thinly sliced, 1 1/2 cups cooked tomatoes instead of water.

DIRECTIONS:
1. Salt ribs. Place in shallow roasting pan, meaty side up.
2. Roast at 450 degrees for 30 minutes.
3. Drain excess fat from pan.
4. Top ribs with sliced, unpeeled lemon and sliced onion.
5. Combine remaining ingredients in medium pot and bring to a boil.
6. Pour over ribs, lower temperature to 350 degrees and bake for another 1 1/2 hours. Make sure you baste ribs with sauce every 15 minutes. If sauce gets too thick, add more water.

BARBECUED PORK CHOPS

TEMP: red hot coals in barbecue
COOKING TIME: 15 minutes each side
PREPARATION TIME: 15 minutes
MAKES: 2 servings

INGREDIENTS:
2 pork chops
7 oz. can tomato sauce
1/2 tsp. sugar
2 cloves garlic, crushed
1/8 tsp. salt
1/8 tsp. pepper

DIRECTIONS:
1. Wash meat under running water before cooking.
2. Mix all ingredients, except meat, in a flat dish.
3. Add pork chops and cover with sauce. Let stand overnight if possible.
4. When ready to barbecue, remove from sauce and cook for at least 30 minutes, turning once or twice.

BARBECUED CHICKEN ===

TEMP: red hot coals in barbecue
COOKING TIME: 20 - 25 minutes each side
PREPARATION TIME: 15 minutes
MAKES: 4 servings

INGREDIENTS:
4 pieces chicken
2 tbsp. oil or butter
1/2 cup barbecue sauce

DIRECTIONS:
1. Rinse chicken.
2. Brush both sides of chicken pieces with oil or butter.
3. Place on barbecue and cook about 30 minutes, turning often, as chicken burns easily.
4. Brush with barbecue sauce and continue cooking another 15 minutes.

BARBECUED FISH STEAKS ===

TEMP: red hot coals in barbecue
COOKING TIME: 15 - 20 minutes
PREPARATION TIME: 15 minutes
MAKES: 3 servings

INGREDIENTS:
3 fish steaks
1 lemon
1/4 cup butter, melted

1/8 tsp. garlic
1/4 tsp. salt
1/4 tsp. pepper

OPTIONAL: Use halibut, cod or salmon fish steaks.

DIRECTIONS:
1. Rinse fish and place on foil.
2. Season with salt and pepper.
3. Cut lemon into wedges and squeeze juice over fish pieces.
4. Mix melted butter with garlic and spoon over fish.
5. Fold foil tightly around fish. Cook approximately 15 - 20 minutes.

FRIED SALMON CUTLETS ════════════

TEMP: medium
COOKING TIME: 10 minutes
PREPARATION TIME: 10 minutes
MAKES: 2 servings

INGREDIENTS:
7 oz. can salmon, drained and deboned
1/2 cup onion, chopped
1/3 cup fine, dry bread crumbs
1 egg, slightly beaten

1/4 tsp. salt
1/8 tsp. pepper
2 tbsp. oil

DIRECTIONS:
1. Drain salmon and flake with fork.
2. Add chopped onion, bread crumbs, egg and seasonings.
3. Mix thoroughly and form into patties.
4. Fry in hot oil, butter, or margarine, until lightly browned.

NOTE: Serve with buttered noodles and salad or steamed vegetables.

EASY BAKED FISH ════════════

TEMP: 375 - 400 degrees
COOKING TIME: 30 minutes
PREPARATION TIME: 5 minutes
MAKES: 4 servings

INGREDIENTS:
1 medium whole fish or 4 fish steaks
1/4 cup mayonnaise
2 tsp. parsley or dill
1/2 tsp. salt
1/4 tsp. pepper

OPTIONAL: Lemon wedges.

DIRECTIONS:
1. Rinse fish.
2. Mix parsley or dill into mayonnaise.
3. Sprinkle salt, pepper and lemon on fish.
4. Spread mayonnaise mixture on fish.
5. Wrap completely in foil and place on baking dish or cookie sheet.
6. Place in oven and bake 30 - 40 minutes.
7. Poke fork into fish. It will be soft and flaky when ready.

BASIC HAMBURGERS

TEMP: Medium
COOKING TIME: 6 - 10 minutes
PREPARATION TIME: 10 minutes
MAKES: 4 servings

INGREDIENTS:

1 lb. ground beef
1/4 cup milk
1/8 tsp. black pepper
1/2 cup bread crumbs or crushed crackers

1 egg
1/2 tsp. salt

OPTIONAL: 1 tbsp. chopped onions

DIRECTIONS:
1. Mix all ingredients well in bowl.
2. Form into 6 - 8 patties.
3. Fry in slightly greased frying pan over medium heat, barbecue or broil about 3 minutes on each side or until cooked.

NOTE: Serve in hamburger bun with onion, cheese, lettuce and tomato or as main dish with vegetables and potatoes. This recipe may also be used to make meatballs or meatloaf.

FRESH LEMON CHICKEN

TEMP: 350 degrees
COOKING TIME: 1 hour
PREPARATION TIME: 5 minutes
MAKES: 4 servings

INGREDIENTS:

4 chicken breasts or 8 drumsticks
juice from 1 lemon
2 tbsp. melted butter

1 tsp. dried tarragon
1/4 tsp. garlic powder

OPTIONAL: 1 tsp. basil in place of tarragon.

DIRECTIONS:
1. Wash chicken.
2. Place chicken in baking dish.
3. Mix lemon juice, butter and spices and pour over chicken.
4. Preheat oven and roast for 45 - 60 minutes.

OVEN FRIED CHICKEN ═══════

TEMP: 375 degrees
COOKING TIME: 1 hour
PREPARATION TIME: 10 minutes
MAKES: 4 servings

INGREDIENTS:

1 cut-up chicken (about 3 lbs.)   1/4 tsp. salt
1/2 cup butter or margarine   dash of pepper
 4 oz. package of potato chips

DIRECTIONS:
1. Wash chicken pieces.
2. Melt butter in small pan.
3. Crush potato chips with rolling pin before opening package.
4. Mix crushed potato chips with garlic salt and pepper on a sheet of wax paper.
5. Dip chicken in melted butter then roll in potato chip crumbs.
6. Place pieces (not touching each other) skin side up on a cookie sheet.
7. Pour the rest of the crumbs over the chicken.
8. Preheat oven and bake for 1 hour.

NOTE: Instead of potato chips, use bread crumbs, corn flakes or crackers.

CHICKEN WITH RICE ═══════

TEMP: low
COOKING TIME: 45 minutes
PREPARATION TIME: 15 minutes
MAKES: 4 servings

INGREDIENTS:

2 tbsp. oil   2 cups water
2 lbs. chicken pieces   3/4 cup uncooked rice
1 package of chicken/onion soup mix

OPTIONAL: 1 cup frozen peas or mixed frozen vegetables.

DIRECTIONS:
1. In large frying pan, brown chicken in hot oil and drain.
2. Add soup mix to water and bring to a boil in frying pan.
3. Stir in rice, vegetables and chicken.
4. Simmer covered, stirring occasionally.
5. Cook for about 45 minutes then check to see if chicken is tender and rice is cooked.

CHICKEN SUPPER IN FRYING PAN ▬▬▬

TEMP: medium - high
COOKING TIME: 30 minutes
PREPARATION TIME: 15 minutes
MAKES: 4 servings

INGREDIENTS:
1 chicken, cut up
3 - 4 potatoes, peeled and cut in half
4 carrots, sliced
10 oz. can cream of mushroom soup

OPTIONAL: Garlic cloves, onions, celery, parsley, herbs or cream of chicken soup.

DIRECTIONS:
1. Wash chicken pieces.
2. Add 1/4 cup oil to frying pan and fry chicken for five minutes on each side on medium heat.
3. Add potatoes, carrots and celery.
4. Add creamed soup diluted with 1/2 cup of water.
5. Mix well.
6. Simmer covered for 1/2 hour.
7. Sprinkle with pepper, parsley and any desired seasonings.

HONEY GLAZED CHICKEN OR RIBS ▬▬▬

TEMP: 350 - 375 degrees
COOKING TIME: 1 hour
PREPARATION TIME: 5 minutes
MAKES: 4 servings

INGREDIENTS:
1 chicken or 2 lbs. ribs
1/2 cup honey
1 cup ketchup
1/4 cup soya sauce
4 cloves garlic, crushed

DIRECTIONS:
1. Wash chicken or ribs under running water.
2. Combine ingredients to make sauce.
3. Place the ribs or chicken pieces in one layer in a roasting pan.
4. Coat with sauce and bake at 350-375 degrees for 1 hour.
5. Baste chicken or ribs occasionally with the sauce while baking.

BAKED CHICKEN ═══════════════════════

TEMP: 350 degrees
COOKING TIME: 2 hours
PREPARATION TIME: 10 minutes
MAKES: 4 - 6 servings

INGREDIENTS:

1 medium chicken (about 3 lbs.)
2 tbsp. barbecue sauce

1/4 tsp. garlic salt
dash of black pepper

DIRECTIONS:
1. Thaw chicken (if frozen).
2. Remove neck and giblets from the cavity.
3. Rinse chicken and blot dry with paper towels.
4. Put chicken onto centre of tin foil sheet (large enough to wrap chicken) and brush on barbecue sauce.
5. Sprinkle chicken with garlic salt and dash of pepper.
6. Wrap tin foil around chicken and put in pan.
7. Bake in preheated oven for 2 hours.

HONEY & MUSTARD CHICKEN ═══════════

TEMP: 350 degrees
COOKING TIME: 1 hour
PREPARATION TIME: 15 minutes
MAKES: 4 servings

INGREDIENTS:

1 frying chicken, cut up and washed
1/4 cup butter
1/2 cup liquid honey

1/4 cup prepared mustard
2 tsp. curry powder

DIRECTIONS:
1. Preheat oven.
2. Put butter in shallow baking pan and put in oven until melted.
3. Remove from oven and add honey, mustard and curry powder, stirring to blend well.
4. Roll chicken pieces in mixture to coat all sides, then put them in pan, meaty side down.
5. Bake 45 minutes, basting often. Turn pieces and bake another 15 minutes or until chicken is tender.

CHINESE CHICKEN WINGS ===

TEMP: 350 degrees
COOKING TIME: 45 minutes
PREPARATION TIME: 1 hour

INGREDIENTS:

approx. 1 1/2 pounds chicken wings
1/4 cup honey
2 tbsp. soya sauce

2 tbsp. lemon juice
1 tsp. garlic salt

OPTIONAL: 3/4 tsp. ginger.

DIRECTIONS:
1. Cut wings into 3 sections (break at joints).
2. Combine rest of ingredients in a saucepan, bring to a boil and let boil for 2 minutes.
3. Place chicken wings in large bowl, pour sauce over wings and place in fridge for at least an hour or overnight.
4. Drain wings and place on cookie sheet or large pan (save sauce).
5. Place in preheated oven. Bake approximately 25 minutes. Baste frequently with extra sauce. Turn chicken wings and bake another 20 minutes. Continue basting with sauce.

PORK CHOP AND POTATO SCALLOP ===

TEMP: 350 degrees
COOKING TIME: 1 hour
PREPARATION TIME: 1/2 hour
MAKES: 3 - 4 servings

INGREDIENTS:

4 pork chops
1 tbsp. oil or margarine
10 oz. can cream of mushroom soup
1/2 cup sour cream

1/4 cup water
4 cups sliced potatoes
salt and pepper to taste

OPTIONAL: 2 tbsp. chopped parsley.

DIRECTIONS:
1. In frying pan, brown chops in oil or margarine.
2. Blend soup, sour cream, water and parsley in bowl.
3. In 2-quart casserole, alternate layers of potatoes, sprinkled with salt, pepper and sauce. Top with chops.
4. Cover and bake for 1 hour.

SPICY BEEF LOG

TEMP: broil
COOKING TIME: 20 minutes
PREPARATION TIME: 20 minutes
MAKES: 4 servings

INGREDIENTS:

1 loaf French bread	1 tsp. oregano
1 1/2 lbs. ground beef	1/8 tsp. pepper
1/2 cup onion, chopped	11 oz. can tomato sauce
2/3 tsp. salt	1/2 cup cheese, grated
2 tbsp. oil	

OPTIONAL: 1 chopped green pepper, 1 tomato.

DIRECTIONS:
1. Cut a trench in French loaf, scoop out bread 1" from edges and about 2" deep.
2. Toast the loaf on a cookie sheet under broiler just until golden.
3. Brown beef in oil in frying pan and drain off fat.
4. Add onion, green pepper, salt, oregano, black pepper and tomato sauce.
5. Simmer 5 -10 minutes.
6. Place filling into trench.
7. Slice one tomato over filling if desired.
8. Sprinkle with cheese.
9. Broil until cheese melts.

NOTE: Toast the scooped out pieces and serve with log or use as croutons.

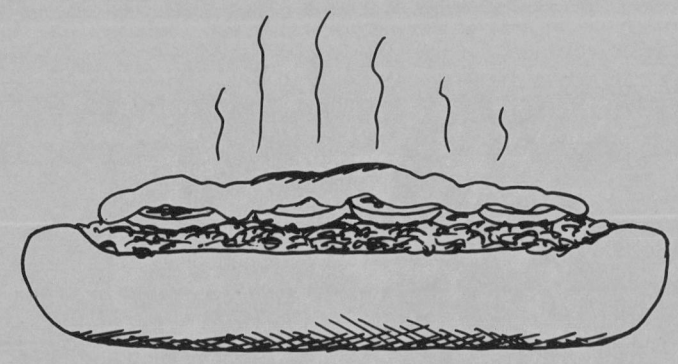

EASY PORK STEAKS AND POTATOES ═══

TEMP: 350 degrees
COOKING TIME: 40 minutes
PREPARATION TIME: 10 minutes
MAKES: 2 servings

INGREDIENTS:

2 - 3 pork steaks
2 - 3 medium potatoes
2 tbsp. sour cream

1 cup cracker crumbs
1 tbsp. cooking oil
1/4 tsp. salt

OPTIONAL: Garlic salt, onion salt, herb seasoning, or shake and bake instead of cracker crumbs.

DIRECTIONS:
1. Trim fat off steaks if desired.
2. Spread sour cream on steaks.
3. Dip in crumbs.
4. Sprinkle with any seasoning.
5. Place on oiled cookie sheet.
6. Peel potatoes and cut in half lengthwise.
7. Place on cookie sheet, next to pork steaks and sprinkle with salt.
8. Bake for 20 minutes, turn and bake another 20 minutes.

CHICKEN A LA MUSHROOM ═══

TEMP: 350 degrees
COOKING TIME: 45 minutes
PREPARATION TIME: 15 minutes
MAKES: 4 - 5 servings

INGREDIENTS:

4 - 5 pieces of chicken
10 oz. can cream of mushroom soup
1 pkg. onion soup mix

1/3 cup milk
1 tbsp. butter

DIRECTIONS:
1. Wash chicken pieces.
2. Arrange chicken in greased casserole.
3. Mix remaining ingredients, pour over chicken.
4. Preheat oven and bake for 45 minutes.

NOTE: Do not use salt.

LOW-BUDGET STEAKS

TEMP: medium
COOKING TIME: 15 minutes
PREPARATION TIME: 15 minutes
MAKES: 6 patties

INGREDIENTS:

1 lb. ground beef
1 tsp. seasoned salt
1 tsp. seasoned or plain pepper
1/2 tbsp. Worcestershire sauce

1 tbsp. vegetable oil
1 tbsp. mustard
1 tbsp. lemon juice
4 tbsp. butter

OPTIONAL: 1/4 cup chopped parsley, pimento or parsley sprigs.

DIRECTIONS:
1. Lightly mix ground beef, salt, and pepper in a bowl. Shape into six 1" thick patties.
2. Melt 2 tbsp. butter in a frying pan, remove from heat, blend in oil and mustard, and return to heat.
3. Saute hamburgers over medium heat, 4 minutes each side for rare.
4. Take patties out of frying pan and place on serving plate.
5. Mix lemon juice, Worcestershire sauce, and remaining 2 tbsp. butter in pan. Stir over low heat until well blended with drippings.
6. Stir in chopped parsley. Spoon over burger steaks.
7. Garnish with pimento and parsley sprigs.

PORK TOFU

TEMP: medium - high
COOKING TIME: 10 minutes
PREPARATION TIME: 10 minutes
MAKES: 3 - 4 servings

INGREDIENTS:

1 lb. pork, cut into pieces
1/2 cup soya sauce
1 1/2 cups water
3 tbsp. sugar
1 tsp. salt

1 onion, thinly sliced
1 pkg. tofu, diced
1 tsp. ginger
3 - 4 green onions, cut
1 tbsp. oil

DIRECTIONS:
1. Saute pork in oil until browned.
2. Combine remaining ingredients, except tofu, in a pot. Bring to a boil.
3. Add pork. Cook for approximately 10 minutes.
4. Reduce heat. Add tofu and simmer approximately 5 minutes.

BEEF STEW

TEMP: 325 degrees
COOKING TIME: 2 hours
PREPARATION TIME: 20 minutes
MAKES: 6 servings

INGREDIENTS:
3 - 4 lbs. stewing beef
1/2 cup flour
6 cloves garlic
1 cup onion, chopped
1 1/2 cups tomato juice or canned tomatoes
2 cubes beef bouillon
   (dissolved in 1 cup hot water)

1/2 cup parsley
1/4 cup vinegar
3 tbsp. brown sugar
1 tsp. salt
1/4 tsp. pepper

DIRECTIONS:
1. Heat oil in Dutch oven or other large pot.
2. Put flour in plastic bag, add beef and shake it to coat with flour.
3. Brown coated beef in oil.
4. Add remaining ingredients, beginning with onions.
5. Mix together and place in oven.
6. Bake at 325 degrees for 2 hours.

VARIATIONS:
Half hour before stew is ready, add:
1 potato, cubed
2 carrots, sliced
12 mushrooms, whole or sliced
6 small onions, whole

Continue to cook untill vegetables are tender.

NOTE: When cutting up vegetables for stew, try to make them all into same size pieces.

SWEET & SOUR CHICKEN DELIGHT ═══

TEMP: 350 degrees
COOKING TIME: 1 hour
PREPARATION TIME: 10 minutes
MAKES: 4 servings

INGREDIENTS:
1 pkg. onion / mushroom soup mix
1/4 cup brown sugar
1/4 cup vinegar
2 lbs. chicken pieces

OPTIONAL: 1/4 cup barbecue sauce may be added to soup, sugar and vinegar mixture. Pork chops may be used instead of chicken.

DIRECTIONS:
1. Preheat oven to 350 degrees.
2. Wash chicken pieces thoroughly.
3 In small bowl combine soup mix, brown sugar and vinegar. Set aside.
4. Place chicken pieces in casserole dish or small roaster and pour soup mixture over chicken.
5. Cover and bake 1 hour.

SWEET & SOUR MEATBALLS ═══

TEMP: 350 degrees
COOKING TIME: 30 minutes
PREPARATION TIME: 15 minutes
MAKES: 4 servings

INGREDIENTS:
1 lb. ground beef
2 tbsp. onions, chopped
1/2 cup dry bread crumbs
1 tbsp. parsley, chopped
1 tsp. garlic salt
1/8 tsp. pepper
1 1/2 tsp. curry powder
1 egg, beaten
2/3 cup milk
2 tbsp. cooking oil

DIRECTIONS:
1. Mix all ingredients (except oil) together.
2. Form into meatballs.
3. Heat oil in pan, add meatballs and brown on all sides.
4. Take out of pan when browned and place in casserole dish.
5 Prepare sweet & sour sauce (see sauces) and pour on meatballs.
6. Bake for 1/2 hour.

CHEESY MEATLOAF

TEMP: 350 degrees
COOKING TIME: 1 hour
PREPARATION TIME: 15 minutes
MAKES: 4 servings

INGREDIENTS:

1 lb. ground beef
1 cup bread crumbs
1/2 cup cheese, cubed
1/2 cup onion, chopped
5 1/2 oz. can tomato sauce

1/4 cup celery
1 1/2 tsp. salt
2 tbsp. ketchup
2 eggs

DIRECTIONS:
1. Combine beef, crumbs, cheese, onions, celery, salt.
2. Beat eggs and tomato sauce together with fork.
3. Add to meat mixture and stir .
4. Place into greased loaf pan or shallow baking dish.
5. Spread ketchup over meatloaf. Bake.

CHILI

TEMP: medium - high
COOKING TIME: 1 hour
PREPARATION TIME: 20 minutes
MAKES: 4 servings

INGREDIENTS:

1 lb. hamburger
1 onion, chopped
1 clove garlic, minced
19 oz. can kidney beans
2 cups canned tomatoes
1 tbsp. vinegar

1/8 cup ketchup
1 tsp. salt
1 tbsp. brown sugar
1 tsp. chili powder
1/4 tsp. dry mustard
1 tbsp. cooking oil

OPTIONAL: 2 tsp. chili sauce, 1/2 a green pepper, chopped,
1/2 tsp. garlic powder instead of garlic clove.

DIRECTIONS:
1. Brown hamburger, onion, green pepper and garlic in oiled pan.
2. Add remaining ingredients and simmer for 1 hour.

OVEN ROAST

TEMP: 325 degrees
TIME: 3 hours (well done), or lower temp. to 225 degrees
and bake for 6 - 8 hours.
PREPARATION TIME: 5 minutes
MAKES: 4 servings

INGREDIENTS:
1 1/2 lb. roast, preferably sirloin tip, rump, or round
(cheaper cut may be used as well, such as cross rib, chuck, etc.)
2 tbsp. onion soup mix
1/2 cup water

DIRECTIONS:
1. Rinse roast (no need to thaw if it's frozen), and put in pan.
2. Add water, and sprinkle with onion soup mix.
3. Cover and bake in 325 degree oven for approximately 3 hours.

NOTE: Cooking time should be reduced to 1 1/2 hours if meat is
thawed or if you prefer rare or medium-rare roast. Add the following to
the roast before baking, for a complete meal all at one time.
2 - 4 peeled potatoes (cut in quarters)
2 - 4 carrots (peeled and cut into 1" pieces
Approximately1 cup whole fresh mushrooms

ROAST BEEF COVERED IN FOIL

TEMP: 375 - 400 degrees
COOKING TIME: 20 - 30 minutes per lb.

INGREDIENTS:
beef roast (sirloin tip, rump, or rolled rump, round)
salt and pepper
seasonings to taste (garlic powder, seasoning salt, onion salt)

DIRECTIONS:
1. Preheat oven to 400 degrees.
2. Wrap meat closely in foil, sealing tightly. Place in pan.
3. Open foil for browning of roast 30 minutes before removing
   from oven.

NOTE: Salt removes moisture from meat during cooking which
can make a roast tough.

SAUCES
GRAVIES
and DIPS

SIMPLE FRENCH DRESSING ═══════

PREPARATION TIME: 5 minutes
MAKES: 1 1/2 cups salad dressing

INGREDIENTS:
1/2 cup salad oil
1/4 cup vinegar
2 tbsp. sugar
1 tbsp. chopped onion
1/2 cup tomato soup

DIRECTIONS:
1. Place all ingredients in blender or jar and mix well.
2. Store in refrigerator.

BASIC WHITE SAUCE ═══════

TEMP: medium
COOKING TIME: 5 minutes
PREPARATION TIME: 3 minutes
MAKES: approximately 1 cup

INGREDIENTS:
1 tbsp. butter or margarine
1 1/2 tbsp. flour
1 cup milk
salt and pepper to taste

DIRECTIONS:
1. Melt butter or margarine in saucepan.
2. Remove from heat and gradually stir in flour.
3. Add 1/4 cup milk to mixture.
4. Stir until smooth. Add remaining milk, stirring constantly.
5. Place saucepan on stove. Stir and cook until sauce thickens (5 minutes.)
6. If sauce is too thin, thicken by adding a little flour. Watch for lumps.

NOTE: Use with vegetables, chicken, seafood, or in casserole dishes.

VARIATION: 4 - 5 tbsp. grated cheddar cheese may be added to make a cheese sauce.

CHEESE SAUCE ═══════════

TEMP: medium
COOKING TIME: approximately 15 minutes
PREPARATION TIME: 5 minutes

INGREDIENTS:
2 tbsp. flour
2 tbsp. butter
1/2 tsp. salt
1 cup milk
1/4 tsp. seasoned salt
4 - 5 slices of cheese, cut up

DIRECTIONS:
1. Combine first 5 ingredients together in a saucepan. Stir with a whisk over medium heat until thickened.
2. Add cut-up cheese slices.
3. Pour over cooked vegetables.

NOTE: Serve over broccoli, carrots, cauliflower, etc.

Too Strong

SWEET & SOUR SAUCE ═══════════

TEMP: medium
COOKING TIME: 5 minutes
PREPARATION TIME: 10 minutes
MAKES: 4 servings

INGREDIENTS:
1/4 cup sugar *(1/2 - 3/4 sugar*
1/2 tsp. salt
20 oz. can pineapple tidbits, drain and save juice *(3/4 c water in place*
1/4 cup vinegar *of juice or*
1 tbsp. soya sauce *just more sugar*
1 tbsp. cornstarch

DIRECTIONS:
1. Mix sugar, salt, and cornstarch in sauce pan.
2. Add pineapple juice, vinegar, and soya sauce to mixture.
3. Bring to a boil. Stir until thick and clear (about 5 minutes).
4. Add pineapple tidbits and pour over meatballs in casserole dish.

LEMON SAUCE

TEMP: medium
COOKING TIME: 15 minutes
PREPARATION TIME: 5 minutes
MAKES: 1 cup

INGREDIENTS:
1/4 cup sugar
2 tbsp. flour or 1 tbsp. cornstarch
1 cup boiling water
1 tbsp. lemon juice
1 tbsp. butter

OPTIONAL: 1 tsp. grated lemon rind.

DIRECTIONS:
1. Mix sugar with flour and add boiling water.
2. Cook 10 -15 minutes.
3. Remove from burner and add butter, lemon juice and rind.
4. Mix well and serve on Brown Betty dessert, brussels sprouts or carrots.

BARBECUE SAUCE

TEMP: medium - high
COOKING TIME: approximately 10 minutes
PREPARATION TIME: 10 minutes
MAKES: 1 1/2 cups

INGREDIENTS:
1/4 cup butter
1/2 cup oil
1/2 cup vinegar
2 tbsp. ketchup
1 tsp. lemon rind, grated

4 tbsp. lemon juice
1 tsp. salt
1/2 tsp. pepper
1/2 tsp. garlic powder

DIRECTIONS:
1. Melt butter over medium heat, add vinegar, oil and ketchup. Mix well.
2. Add all other ingredients.
3. Bring to a boil and remove from heat.
4. Store in fridge.

RAISIN SAUCE (For Ham)

TEMP: medium
COOKING TIME: 10 minutes
PREPARATION TIME: 5 minutes
MAKES: approximately 2 cups

INGREDIENTS:

1/2 cup brown sugar
1 tsp. dry mustard
2 tbsp. cornstarch
2 tbsp. vinegar

2 tbsp. lemon juice
1 1/2 cups water
1/2 cup raisins

DIRECTIONS:
1. Mix brown sugar, mustard and cornstarch in saucepan.
2. Add vinegar, lemon juice, water and raisins.
3. Cook over medium heat, constantly stirring until sauce thickens.
4. Spoon over cooked ham.

MEATLESS SPAGHETTI SAUCE

TEMP: medium
COOKING TIME: 15 to 20 minutes
PREPARATION TIME: 15 minutes
MAKES: 6 servings

INGREDIENTS:

1 tbsp. butter
1 medium onion, chopped
10 oz. can tomato soup
2 tbsp. barbecue sauce or ketchup
1/2 cup water

2 cloves garlic, minced
1/2 tsp. oregano
1/2 tsp. salt
1/8 tsp. pepper

OPTIONAL: 1 cup sliced mushrooms (canned or fresh).

DIRECTIONS:
1. Melt butter in pan.
2. Add chopped onion. Saute.
3. Add mushrooms and continue to saute.
4. Add remaining ingredients.
5. Simmer 15 - 20 minutes.

NOTE: Almost anything goes with spaghetti sauce so don't be afraid to experiment!

SUPER EASY SPAGHETTI SAUCE

TEMP: medium - high
COOKING TIME: 20 minutes
PREPARATION TIME: 10 minutes
MAKES: 4 servings

INGREDIENTS:

15 oz. can tomato sauce
1 lb. hamburger
salt and pepper to taste

1/4 tsp. garlic powder
2 tbsp. oil
1/4 tsp. oregano

OPTIONAL: 1/4 cup chopped green pepper, 1/4 cup chopped onion,
1/2 cup chopped mushrooms, 1/4 cup chopped celery.

DIRECTIONS:
1. Heat oil in large frying pan.
2. Add hamburger, salt, pepper, garlic powder, green pepper, onion,
   mushrooms and celery and saute until hamburger browns.
3. Add tomato sauce and oregano and simmer for 10 minutes.
4. Serve over cooked spaghetti.

SPAGHETTI SAUCE

TEMP: medium
COOKING TIME: 30 minutes
PREPARATION TIME: 15 minutes
MAKES: 4 servings

INGREDIENTS:

1/2 lb. hamburger
10 oz. can mushrooms, sliced
1/2 cup green pepper, chopped

1/2 tsp. salt
14 oz. can spaghetti sauce
1 tbsp. cooking oil

DIRECTIONS:
1. Heat oil in large pan. Add hamburger and stir until browned.
2. Add spaghetti sauce, mushrooms, green pepper and garlic salt.
3. Simmer on medium to low heat for 1/2 hour, stirring occasionally.
4. Serve over cooked spaghetti.

BEAN DIP

TEMP: 350 degrees
COOKING TIME: 5 minutes
PREPARATION TIME: 5 minutes

INGREDIENTS:

2 small cans bean dip
  (or 14 oz. can refried beans)
1 cup sour cream
1 cup cheddar cheese, grated

1 1/2 oz. taco mix
1 small onion, chopped
10 drops Tabasco sauce
8 oz. cream cheese

DIRECTIONS:

1. Mix everything together in blender.
2. Pour into baking dish.
3. Top with cheese.
4. Bake until cheese melts.
5. Serve with tortilla chips.

BASIC ONION DIP ══════════════

PREPARATION TIME: 2 minutes
MAKES: 2 1/2 cups

INGREDIENTS:
1 package onion soup mix
1 pint sour cream

DIRECTIONS:
1. Combine onion soup mix and sour cream.
2. Cover and refrigerate for at least 1 hour before serving.

NOTE: Serve with potato chips or raw vegetables.

POULTRY GRAVY ══════════════

TEMP: medium
COOKING TIME: 10 minutes
PREPARATION TIME: 10 minutes
MAKES: 2 cups

INGREDIENTS:

4 tbsp. butter or margarine	1/2 cup milk
4 tbsp. all purpose flour	1/2 cup poultry drippings
1 tsp. onion, chopped	1 chicken bouillon cube
1/4 cup mushrooms, chopped	1 clove garlic, crushed
salt to taste	3/4 cup water, boiling

OPTIONAL: 1/2 cup light cream instead of milk.

DIRECTIONS:
1. Melt butter in saucepan.
2. Saute onion and mushrooms for 5 minutes.
3. Add flour and stir over medium heat until bubbly.
4. Dissolve chicken boullion cube in water.
5. Stir in milk or cream, drippings, bouillon, garlic and salt.
6. Cook over medium heat, stirring constantly until gravy thickens.

NOTE: Delicious over chicken or turkey. Use leftover gravy on hot chicken or turkey sandwiches. (Also great over mashed potatoes.)

GRAVY

TEMP: medium
COOKING TIME: 3 - 5 minutes
PREPARATION TIME: 3 minutes
MAKES: 1 cup

INGREDIENTS:
2 tbsp. meat drippings
2 tbsp. flour
1 cup water
salt and pepper to taste

DIRECTIONS:
1. Put drippings into small pan.
2. Mix water and flour together (smooth out as many lumps as possible).
3. Add this mixture to meat drippings, put pan on low heat and stir until gravy thickens. Salt and pepper to taste.

CREOLE GRAVY

TEMP: medium - high
COOKING TIME: 15 minutes
PREPARATION TIME: 10 minutes
MAKES: enough gravy for 1 pound of meatloaf

INGREDIENTS:
1 1/2 green peppers, chopped
1 tbsp. butter or margarine
1 package light brown gravy mix
1 medium onion, chopped
salt and pepper to taste
7 oz. can mushrooms (stems and pieces)

DIRECTIONS:
1. Melt butter in medium-sized saucepan.
2. Saute mushrooms, peppers and onions (approximately 5 minutes).
3. Mix gravy with water according to package directions.
4. Add gravy to vegetables and simmer for 5 minutes, then pour over meatloaf.

DESSERTS

CHOCOLATE CHIP COOKIES ▬▬▬

TEMP: 350 degrees
COOKING TIME: 10 minutes
PREPARATION TIME: 10 minutes
MAKES: 30 cookies

INGREDIENTS:

1/2 cup butter or margarine
1/2 cup brown sugar
1 egg, beaten
1 tsp. vanilla

1 1/8 cup sifted flour
1/4 tsp. baking soda
3/4 cup chocolate chips
1/2 cup walnuts, chopped

DIRECTIONS:
1. Cream butter and sugar together.
2. Add egg and vanilla.
3. Blend thoroughly.
4. Sift flour, soda and salt in separate bowl.
5. Add sifted ingredients to egg/butter mixture.
6. Fold in nuts and chocolate chips.
7. Drop from teaspoon onto greased baking sheet.
8. Bake for 10 minutes or until nicely browned.

PEANUT BUTTER COOKIES ▬▬▬

TEMP: 350 degrees
COOKING TIME: 12 - 15 minutes per pan
PREPARATION TIME: 10 minutes
MAKES: approx. 2 dozen

INGREDIENTS:

1/2 cup brown sugar
1/2 cup white sugar
1/2 cup butter or margarine
1 cup peanut butter
1 egg

1/2 tsp. vanilla
1 1/2 cups flour
1/2 tsp salt
1/2 tsp. baking soda

DIRECTIONS:
1. Cream butter, sugars and peanut butter.
2. Add egg and vanilla.
3. Blend in flour, salt and baking soda.
4. Shape into 1" balls, flatten with fork and bake for 12 - 15 minutes on greased cookie sheet.

GIANT OATMEAL COOKIES

TEMP: 375 degrees
COOKING TIME: 10 minutes per pan
PREPARATION TIME: 20 minutes
MAKES: 12

INGREDIENTS:
1/2 cup butter or margarine
1/2 cup white sugar
1/2 cup packed brown sugar
1 large egg
1 tsp. vanilla
1 cup all purpose flour

1 tsp. ground cinnamon
1/2 tsp. baking powder
1/2 tsp. baking soda
1/4 tsp. salt
1 cup quick-cooking oats

OPTIONAL: 1/3 cup raisins, 1 cup chocolate chips.

DIRECTIONS:
1. Preheat oven to 375 degrees.
2. Put butter, sugars, egg and vanilla into a large bowl. Beat until creamy.
3. Add flour, cinnamon, baking powder, baking soda and salt to the bowl. Beat until well blended.
4. Add oats, raisins and chocolate chips. Mix well.
5. Roll batter into balls, using 1/4 cup batter for each ball. Place on well-greased cookie sheet. Bake on middle rack for 10 -12 minutes or until golden.

MOLASSES BUTTERBALL COOKIES

TEMP: 325 degrees
COOKING TIME: 20 minutes
PREPARATION TIME: 10 minutes
MAKES: 4 dozen

INGREDIENTS:
1 cup margarine
2 cups finely chopped walnuts

2 cups flour
1/4 cup molasses

DIRECTIONS:
1. Preheat oven.
2. Combine all ingredients and mix well.
3. Use 1 tsp. of dough for each cookie. Shape into balls.
4. Place dough on ungreased cookie sheet and bake for 20 minutes.
5. When cool, roll in powdered icing sugar.

PEANUT BUTTER CHEWS

TEMP: low
COOKING TIME: 10 minutes
PREPARATION TIME: 10 minutes
MAKES: 24 - 1 1/2" squares

INGREDIENTS:

1 cup peanut butter
1/2 cup corn syrup
1/2 cup brown sugar

1 tsp. vanilla
3 cups Rice Krispies
1 tbsp. butter or margarine

DIRECTIONS:
1. Combine peanut butter, corn syrup, brown sugar and vanilla in a saucepan.
2. Place over low heat and stir until melted and combined.
3. Remove from heat and stir in Rice Krispies until coated with peanut butter mixture.
4. Press into a greased 8" square pan and chill 1 hour in fridge.
5. Cut into squares.

DAD'S COOKIES

TEMP: 375 degrees
COOKING TIME: approximately 10 minutes
PREPARATION TIME: 15 minutes
MAKES: 5 dozen

INGREDIENTS:

1 cup butter or margarine
2 eggs
2 cups flour
1 tsp. baking powder
2 cups rolled oats
1 cup chocolate chips

2 cups brown sugar
1 tsp. vanilla
1/2 tsp. baking soda
1/4 tsp. salt
1 1/2 cups fine coconut

DIRECTIONS:
1. Cream together butter and sugar.
2. Add beaten eggs and vanilla.
3. Sift dry ingredients and add to egg mixture.
4. Add oats, coconut and chips and mix well.
5. Roll into balls and press down with fork dipped in water.
6. Bake.

REFRIGERATOR BRAN MUFFINS

TEMP: 350 degrees
PREPARATION TIME: 10 minutes
BAKING TIME: 20 - 25 minutes
MAKES: 18 muffins

INGREDIENTS:
1 cup buttermilk
1 cup bran
1 egg
1/3 cup oil
1/3 cup brown sugar
1/3 cup white sugar

1 tsp. baking soda
2/3 tsp. salt
1/2 tsp. vanilla
1/3 cup raisins
1 cup flour
1 tsp. baking powder

DIRECTIONS:
1. Mix buttermilk and bran. Let stand.
2. Mix egg, oil, sugars, soda, salt, vanilla and raisins.
3. Mix flour and baking powder.
4. Mix bran mixture with the liquid mixture.
5. Quickly mix in the flour mixture.
6. Fill greased muffin cups 3/4 full with batter.
7. Bake for 20 - 25 minutes.

NOTE: This muffin mixture can be kept in the refrigerator for up to three weeks and baked fresh as needed.

TOASTED MALLOW PUDDING

TEMP: broiler
COOKING TIME: 5 minutes
PREPARATION TIME: 30 minutes
MAKES: 4 servings

INGREDIENTS:
1 (106 gram) pkg. instant pudding (any flavour)
1 1/2 cups miniature marshmallows
2 cups milk

DIRECTIONS:
1. Prepare pudding as directed on package.
2. Pour pudding into a 1-quart heat-proof serving dish.
3. Chill for about 20 minutes or until firm.
4. Sprinkle marshmallows over pudding at serving time.
5. Broil until marshmallows are golden brown.

QUICK PUDDING PARFAITS ════════

PREPARATION TIME: 15 minutes
MAKES: 4 servings

INGREDIENTS:
106 gram package instant vanilla pudding
1 3/4 cups milk
1 cup whipping cream
3/4 tsp. vanilla
1 1/2 cups strawberries, bananas or other fruit

DIRECTIONS:
1. Prepare pudding according to directions on package,except use only 1 3/4 cups of milk.
2. Whip cream until stiff.
3. Fold whipped cream and vanilla into pudding.
4. Slice fruit.
5. Layer pudding and fruit in parfait glasses, or any dessert dish.
6. Chill until serving time.

APPLE CRISP ════════════

TEMP: 350 degrees
COOKING TIME: 45 minutes
PREPARATION TIME: 15 minutes
MAKES: 4 servings

INGREDIENTS:

5 cups sliced apples	1 cup brown sugar
3/4 cup flour	3/4 cup oatmeal
1 tsp. cinnamon	1/2 cup butter

DIRECTIONS:
1. Peel and slice apples and put into 1-quart casserole dish.
2. Add brown sugar and mix well.
3. Combine flour, oatmeal and cinnamon. Add butter.
4. Mix until crumbly.
5. Sprinkle flour mixture on top of apples and bake for about 45 minutes.

PINEAPPLE FROST ======

PREPARATION TIME: 15 minutes
MAKES: 4 servings

INGREDIENTS:
14 oz. can frozen pineapple chunks
1/2 cup shredded or flaked coconut
1 banana, sliced
1 pint fresh strawberries

DIRECTIONS:
1. Let can of pineapple chunks stand at room temperature about 1 hour.
2. Wash berries, take off stems. Cut berries in half.
3. Lightly toss strawberries, bananas, pineapple and coconut.
4. Spoon into dessert dishes.
5. Serve while pineapple is still frosty.

EASY CHEESECAKE ======

TEMP: 350 degrees
COOKING TIME: 30 minutes
PREPARATION TIME: 15 minutes
MAKES: 9 servings

INGREDIENTS:
1/4 cup sugar
1 1/2 cups graham crumbs
1/3 cup softened butter
8 oz. cream cheese
19 oz. can blueberry or cherry pie filling

1 tsp vanilla
1/2 cup sugar
2 eggs
1 cup Cool Whip

DIRECTIONS:
1. Mix sugar, graham crumbs and butter.
2. Press into 8" x 8" pan.
3. Bake in 350 degree oven for 5 minutes.
4. Mix together eggs, cream cheese, vanilla and sugar.
5. Pour over crust.
6. Bake another 20 minutes.
7. Cool.
8. Top with blueberry or cherry pie filling.

NOTE: May be served with or without whipped topping.

ROCKY ROAD CAKE ═══════════

TEMP: low
COOKING TIME: 10 minutes
PREPARATION TIME: 20 minutes
MAKES: 24 squares

INGREDIENTS:
6 oz. butterscotch chips
1/2 cup margarine
1 cup icing sugar
1 egg
2 cups miniature marshmallows
16 graham wafers, approximately
1/4 cup coconut

DIRECTIONS:
1. Line a 9" x 9" pan with graham wafers.
2. Melt the chips and margarine on low heat.
3. Add icing sugar and egg to mixture, stir until thickened.
4. Cool slighty.
5. Add marshmallows and mix, then spread on top of wafers.
6. Sprinkle with fine or medium coconut.

LAZY DAY CHOCOLATE CAKE ═══════════

PREPARATION TIME: 5 minutes
BAKING TIME: 30 - 35 minutes
TEMP: 350 degrees
MAKES: 1 small cake

INGREDIENTS:
1 1/2 cups flour
1 cup sugar
3 tbsp. cocoa
1 tsp. baking soda
1/2 tsp. salt

1 cup water
6 tbsp. cooking oil
1 tbsp. vinegar or
   lemon juice

DIRECTIONS:
1. Sift first five ingredients together.
2. Empty into ungreased 8" x 8" cake pan, or something similar.
3. Add water, oil and vinegar to ingredients in pan.
4. Stir vigorously with fork until all mix is moistened (1 to 1 1/2 minutes).
5. Bake 30 - 35 min. or until cake springs back when lightly pressed.
6. Cool and eat--no need for icing.

BROWN BETTY

TEMP: 325 degrees
COOKING TIME: 45 minutes
PREPARATION TIME: 20 minutes
MAKES: 4 - 6 servings

INGREDIENTS:

1/4 cup sugar
1/4 tsp. cinnamon
1/2 tsp. lemon rind, grated
2 cups bread or graham
   cracker crumbs

3 cups sliced apples
1/4 cup butter
2 tbsp. lemon juice
1/2 cup cold water

OPTIONAL: Any ripe berries may be substituted for apples.

DIRECTIONS:
1. Preheat oven.
2. Peel and slice apples.
3. Mix sugar, cinnamon, lemon juice and rind.
4. Melt butter and mix with crumbs.
5. Butter an 8" x 8" baking pan or a 1-quart casserole.
6. Put in one quarter of crumb mixture into bottom of pan, top with one half of apples and sprinkle with half of the sugar mixture.
7. Put another layer of crumbs, apple and sugar mixture and sprinkle remaining crumbs on top.
8. Add water and bake, covered, for about 30 minutes.
9. When apples are soft, remove cover and brown the crumbs (about 15 minutes). Serve with cream or lemon sauce (see sauces).

JELLY ICE CREAM DESSERT

PREPARATION TIME: 10 minutes
MAKES: 6 servings

INGREDIENTS:
85 gram box jelly powder (any flavour)
1 cup water
2 cups vanilla ice cream

DIRECTIONS:
1. Boil water.
2. Add jelly powder to water and stir until dissolved.
3. Add ice cream by spoonfuls, mixing until smooth.
4. Refrigerate until firm.

CHERRY DELIGHT

PREPARATION TIME: 30 minutes
MAKES: approximately 12 squares

INGREDIENTS:
1 1/2 cups graham wafers, crushed
1/4 cup melted butter
4 oz. cream cheese or cottage cheese
1/2 cup icing sugar
1 tsp. vanilla
1 cup whipping cream
19 oz. can cherry pie filling

DIRECTIONS:
1. Mix graham wafers and melted butter.
2. Put into 9" x 9" dish.
3. Whip cream.
4. Mix cream cheese, icing sugar and vanilla with whipped cream.
5. Pour over graham crust.
6. Gently spread cherry pie filling over top.
7. Store in refrigerator.

RICE KRISPY SQUARES

PREPARATION TIME: 10 minutes
MAKES: approximately 16 pieces

INGREDIENTS:
1/4 cup butter
5 cups Rice Krispies
16 oz. package marshmallows

DIRECTIONS:
1. Melt butter.
2. Add marshmallows to butter. Cook over low heat until melted.
3. Remove from heat and add Rice Krispies. Stir.
4. Press into buttered 9" x 9" pan.
5. Put in fridge for at least 1 hour and cut when ready to eat.

PUFFED WHEAT SQUARES ═══

TEMP: medium
COOKING TIME: 10 minutes
PREPARATION TIME: 15 minutes
MAKES: 15 squares

INGREDIENTS:
1/2 cup corn syrup
1/3 cup margarine
1 cup brown sugar
1 tsp. vanilla
2 tbsp cocoa
8 cups puffed wheat

DIRECTIONS:
1. Melt margarine in small pot.
2. Add syrup, sugar, cocoa and vanilla.
3. Cook, stirring frequently, until bubbles begin to form.
4. Remove from heat.
5. Pour over puffed wheat and stir until well coated.
6. Butter a 9" x 12" pan.
7. Pat puffed wheat mixture into pan.
8. Cut into squares and serve.

ICE CREAM ═══

PREPARATION TIME: 15 minutes
MAKES: 2 - 4 servings

INGREDIENTS:
1 egg
1/8 tsp. salt
1 tbsp. vanilla
1/2 cup sugar
1 2/3 cups of light cream (half and half)

DIRECTIONS:
1. Beat the egg.
2. Add remaining ingredients and beat well.
3. Freeze and eat!

NOTES

INDEX